Greetings from
High School

THE PETERSON'S H.S. SERIES
Books by, for, and about teens

Greetings from High School
Teenspeak About High School and Life

War and Peace in the Persian Gulf:
What Teenagers Want to Know
(A "Peterson's H.S." Special Report)

150 Ways Teens Can Make a Difference
Strategies for Making a Genuine Contribution

Greetings from
High School

by Marian Salzman and Teresa Reisgies
with Ann O'Reilly

and

David Portny '90, Dale Allsopp '91,
Ashley Bryan '92, Caroline Portny '94,
and Amanda Abraham '95

Also with

Kathryn Alexander, Jessica Berkeley, Tara Bradley,
Meredyth Cohn, Victoria DeFrance, Dan Diman, Meraiah Foley,
Kyle Galloway, Tony George, Adam Goodman, Alieda Hempstead,
Andrew Hunter, Mindy Jones, Toi Jones, Adam Kanner, Kirk Kenfield,
Brian Klugman, Alexandra Marrufo, Melissa Marshall, Alexandra Meckel,
Emily Miller, Ryan Nelson, Ron Palmon, Vinod Paul, Alex Quintero,
Sarah Ribbeck, Colin Robinson, Maria Rosel, Jamie Sattel, Joey Schmidt,
Zoe Schonfeld, Leo Shin, Rachel Smith, Rebecca Stevens, Jamie Stover,
Lawrence Thaler, Bryan and Matthew Thanner, Jeff Toohig,
Tracy Weinberg, Dana Wolf, Nancy Wong,

and several thousand other teenage contributors

Peterson's Guides
Princeton, New Jersey

 TEXT PRINTED ON RECYCLED PAPER

Library of Congress Cataloging-in-Publication Data

Salzman, Marian, 1959–
    Greetings from high school / by Marian Salzman and Teresa Reisgies with
Ann O'Reilly ... [et al.].
        p. cm.
    Includes index.
    Summary: Discusses what life is like in high school, covering such aspects
as stress, schoolwork, family, romance, and sports.
    ISBN 1-56079-055-5
    1. High school students — United States — Conduct of life. 2. Teenagers
— United States — Conduct of life. 3. High schools — United States —
Juvenile literature. [1. High schools. 2. Schools.] I. Reisgies, Teresa, 1966– .
II. O'Reilly, Ann. III. Title.
BJ1661.S25 1991
373.18 — dc20   91-6868

Cover and text design by Frierson + Mee Associates, Inc.

Printed in the United States of America

10 9 8 7 6 5 4 3 2 1

To our high school administrators, friends, and teachers — and our families — because you're the ones who gave us the memories.

Contents

Preface

Last April, I got a call from Peter Hegener, whom I have known for several years. Would I be interested in meeting with Peterson's Guides' new editorial director to talk about collaborating on some books? A week later I had lunch with Judy Garodnick, and, voilà, this book — and the entire "Peterson's H.S." series — was born over salads in Princeton, New Jersey.

Between May and October I spent countless hours talking with high school students and working alongside my best sources: Amanda Abraham, Ashley Bryan, and David and Caroline Portny. Dale Allsopp, Rachel Smith, and so many other kids also taught me a great deal. Each one of them reminded me how little has really changed since the days when I headed to high school each morning. I still remember the moment when the book came together for me. Ashley and her friend Luisa Feagin from Texas were in the office; so were David and Amanda. We all sat around the conference table for hours, as they explained what was what in high school. Boy, did the talk sound familiar.

Sure, the battles with administrators about recycling were new themes, but the *modus operandi* for social change wasn't very different. As we were finishing, Ashley summed things up brilliantly when she said something to the effect of, "We're very anxious to grow up and we're very worried about our futures, but we also want to help other people and want to make a difference in this world. We're not selfish, but we are practical. We don't like to waste time. We study hard, we like to party, and we also like to do the right thing. We respect our parents because we understand the sacrifices they've made for us. We're not angry or rebellious like previous generations, but we do fight for things we believe in." This philosophy has been confirmed again and again by literally thousands of students we've met or who have written to us. (Thank you, Ashley, for getting it right the first time.)

This brief explanation wouldn't be complete without a word about the special role David Portny played in this book. I've known David for two years, since he was a high school junior, and his insights and perspective figure heavily in this book. To say that he is levelheaded is to underestimate him. This guy manages to turn acquaintances into friends in about two seconds. He and Terry Barnett, my assistant, visited summer camps and brought back the names of dozens of kids who wanted to help — and more ideas than we could possibly accommodate in one book. In fact, David Portny's attitudes about community service were the initial inspiration for the second book in the "Peterson's H.S." series, *150 Ways Teens Can Make a Difference*. (Over the course of compiling *Greetings from High School*, many other students we met across the country also spoke about just how important community service is to them.)

Finally, I need to explain that my interest in junior high and high school students has been greatly encouraged by the kids I've gotten to know during these past few years. Alexandra Meckel and Caroline Portny, especially, have constantly reminded me that being a teenager is full of trials and tribulations, as well as fantastic opportunities. When else in one's life do you have the kinds of confidants and friends these two have? We can all learn a lesson about friendship from watching teenage best friends relate to one another with such care and consideration. Of course, their parents bear the brunt of their addiction to the telephone. . . .

ACKNOWLEDGMENTS

Special thanks to Donna Zaccaro, Terry Barnett, Cindy Lane Fazio, and Cordelia Richards of The Bedford Kent Group; to Gary Goldstein and his colleagues at The Whitney Group; to Rick Salomon of Christy & Viener; to Geraldine Ferraro for her keynote address at the first annual National Teenage Summit, the round of meetings held in conjunction with this book in October in New York City; to Peter and Casey Hegener of Peterson's Guides, and to Judy Garodnick, editorial director, and Eric Newman, senior developmental editor, of Peterson's Guides.

Special thanks also to our friends Warner Johnson, Lori Macleod, Bill Meckel, David Ronick, and Arlene Stiller, who chaperoned the teenage delegates during the summit weekend, and to Deidre Sullivan for the insights she shared with the delegates prior to the publication of her new book, *What Do We Mean When We Say God?* (Doubleday, 1991). The following establishments in New York City were gracious to our visiting delegates: Bueno Gusto Café, Dallas Barbeque, Hwa Yuan Szechuan Inn, and Squid Roe. And special thanks to The Birch Wathen School.

Special thanks also to George Gurley, a senior at the University of Kansas who developed a "hit list" of schools for us to contact and who contributed to the chapter called "We Are the World." We're also grateful to the following schools, which encouraged their students to participate in our data-collection efforts: Brooks School, North Andover, Massachusetts; The Calhoun School, New York, New York; Crystal Springs Upland School, Hillsborough, California; Dwight Englewood School, Englewood, New Jersey; Hampton Roads Academy, Newport News, Virginia; Harpeth Hall School, Nashville, Tennessee; Harrells Christian Academy, Harrells, North Carolina; Indian Springs School, Helena, Alabama; The Louisville Collegiate School, Louisville, Kentucky; Manchester Memorial High School, Manchester, New Hampshire; The Maret School, Washington, D.C.; Oregon Episcopal School, Portland, Oregon; Squaw Valley Academy, Olympic Valley, California; and Thomas More Prep–Marian High, Hays, Kansas. We also appreciate the efforts of the following students, who organized focus group meetings at their schools: Kelly Nordlinger, The Bullis School, Potomac, Maryland; Tracy Pruzan, The Sidwell Friends School, Washington, D.C.; and Keelyn Welch, Swampscott High School, Swampscott, Massachusetts.

Finally, a number of summer camps graciously allowed us to talk with their teenage campers last summer: Camp Netimus, Milford, Pennsylvania; Camp Pasquaney, Bristol, New Hampshire; Camp Shohola, Greeley, Pennsylvania; Camp Susquehannock for Girls, Friendsville, Pennsylvania; Camp Timber Tops, Greeley, Pennsylvania; Interlocken International Summer Camp, Hillsboro Upper Village, New Hampshire; and Pine Forest Camp, Greeley, Pennsylvania. Thanks also to Bill Cole of Peterson's Guides, who opened these and lots of other doors for us.

Marian Salzman
March 1991

Introduction

**"This past year I moved from Nashville to Knoxville
and transferred to a larger public school. I'm learning
how to think, not to take everything at face value.
It's more than just what I learn in my classes.
I have begun to interact with different kinds of people
and to investigate different ways of thinking."**

Kathryn Alexander, an eleventh grader at Bearden
High School in Knoxville, Tennessee

Nobody likes to hear about the Dark Ages. Think how quickly you begin to roll your eyes when your parents or teachers start in about what life was like when they were your age. Still, bear with me for just a minute or two. First, I'm not quite old enough to be your parent, and I'm certainly not patient enough to be your teacher. Second, I think my own high school experience isn't all that different from what so many of you will encounter. Third, this is a perfect opportunity to settle a score. When all those teachers gave me B's instead of A's (and occasionally a C or D in chemistry, math, or physics), I swore that someday I'd prove they had underestimated me. I have yet to win the Nobel Prize for physics, but recounting my version of the dos and don'ts of high school will still be sweet revenge.

I graduated from River Dell Regional High School in Oradell, New Jersey, in 1977 — not so very long ago. Strangely, I can't remember my first day there. I can't even remember whether we shifted buildings at the end of eighth grade or at the end of ninth. What I do remember is exactly what I wore for the first three days of seventh grade — down to the color

1

of my socks and the fact that my shoes were two-tone (a.k.a. "saddle"). I also remember, perfectly, the last day of eighth grade.

I used to hang with a group of girls known as "The Brunettes." One night, during the summer between eighth and ninth grades, they tried to make me an honorary brunette by shoe polishing my blond hair. Needless to say, my mother was thrilled. The Brunettes hung around with a group of guys — I think they called themselves "The Sea Men." Every Friday night, and lots of Saturdays, we went to parties at somebody's house, preferably without parents on the premises. We listened to music, on occasion we drank beer, but, all in all, we were good kids. We wanted to go to college or begin careers, we cared about our school, and we took pride in serving it as athletes, as class and student government officers, as journalists on the school paper. We rebelled, but somehow our actions always stayed within mildly acceptable boundaries. Perhaps it was because we were forward-thinking: Without talking about it, we all seemed to recognize that if we got nailed for doing something seriously unacceptable, we would lose out on all that lay ahead. We would be removed from the great race before we'd made it halfway around the track.

Don't get me wrong. Lots of us related better to Holden Caulfield, the rebel you'll soon read about in *The Catcher in the Rye,* than we did to our parents, or even to one another, but we stuck together through good times and bad. We studied hard some of the time, but we also skipped as many classes as we could, digging up every possible excuse, from a sore throat waiting to happen to an important meeting with the dentist. At one time or another, each of us managed to experience a flat tire in transit.

In suburban and rural areas, the high school years break down into two key phases: BC and WDL — that is, "before cars" and "with driver's license." The sixteenth (or fifteenth or seventeenth) birthday is the magical time when you're first eligible for a license. You're a free man or woman. No more depending on car pools and school buses, no more hitching rides with older friends and siblings, and no more wasted time persuading your parents to don their chauffeurs' caps.

Even if you're rarely allowed to borrow the family wheels, chances are one of your friends has access to a set. I remember the sense of exhilaration I felt when my mother first handed me the car keys — to a beat-up Plymouth, mind you — and I was off. It was the spring of my junior year. Was I psyched! Even though I had sworn to her that I wouldn't, I blared the radio, hit the gas pedal hard, and headed for school with screeching tires. (Of course, I'm not advocating that you begin your celebration the way I did on this, the second best day of my high school career.)

2

The best day of high school started out in the post office. It was mid-April, and college acceptances were beginning to trickle in. Like any racer in the last lap, I was pumped and scared to death. I had applied to half a dozen schools, maybe more. Each morning that week, I called the post office and stopped mail delivery to my house. (That way I had access to the day's mail by 8:30 A.M. instead of having to wait until I got home from school.)

On that fateful day in April, the line at the post office was long. I was wearing white cotton shorts, long ones, and a red-and-white-striped T-shirt. My shoes were black leather pumps. Can you believe that I remember every detail about the outfit I wore to get the news?

When I got to the front of the line, the clerk handed me envelopes from Yale, Mount Holyoke, and Brown. The first two were thin. The last one was fat. I tore open the fat one first and saw "I am pleased to . . ." That was it. I had passed "Go," and my life was proceeding as planned.

Whether or not I'd like to admit it to you up front, the truth is that my high school years were made when I got into a good college. (My friends who opted against college say they felt the same way once they managed to line up a postgraduation job.) The last two months were bliss. All the bad times were forgotten, and it was one rally on Easy Street. Somehow, all the years spent going to classes, doing homework, and putting up with the hassles that came with living with my family seemed worthwhile. In fact, even the three nights and all day Saturday I spent each week working behind the counter at Bedazzle, a local jewelry store, no longer fazed me. I had been accepted at a good college. Who cared how much time I had to spend sitting in the window of Bedazzle making customized baby bracelets — the 1976 equivalent of today's surfer bracelets.

Now that I'm older and, I hope, a bit wiser, I can honestly report, though, that although Brown sure was a great place to go to college, there's nothing like those four years I spent in high school. For me, high school was the place in which I learned about life and about love. It's where I learned to love my life. It's also where I learned how to face adversity and disappointments and — perhaps the greatest lesson of all — how to keep a sense of perspective regardless of how tough the going gets. In so many ways, high school is a race toward the future, but in the end it's the race itself that counts the most.

So now that I've bored you with my quick sprint down memory lane (at least I didn't insist that the publisher include yearbook pics of my nearest and dearest pals), I hope you're psyched to find out everything you ever wanted to know about the fast time you're likely to experience at Every High School, Anytown, U.S.A.

Before I get to your questions, there's just one more thing I'd like to tell you. The only regret I have about high school doesn't have very much to do with high school at all.

On the last day of eighth grade, my English teacher (I think her name was Barnes) asked us to write letters to ourselves. She told us she would mail the letters to us in four years, on the day we graduated from high school. I spent hours working on mine. I asked questions about the family dog, Charlie, who would die the summer after junior year; about whether my parents had ended up getting a divorce (they didn't, and in retrospect I wonder why I even considered the possibility); about my then best friend, Jeanne Mersch, who would move away shortly thereafter; and about an exchange student who was spending a month with us that summer. Well, I never received the letter. I waited for it for weeks and was devastated when it didn't arrive. (Ever the optimist, I even hoped that it would show up in 1981, four years later. I tried to convince myself that I had misunderstood and that she was mailing the letters when we were leaving college, instead. Wrong.)

Anyway, my best suggestion to you is that when you finish reading this book and you get all revved up about high school, sit down and write yourself a letter. Tell yourself what you're like now. Forecast where you think you'll be in four years. Record details: feelings, people, places. Believe me when I say that you'll appreciate this letter more than any other graduation gift you'll receive — even more than the cash. I promise. Now, on to the race.

HIGH SCHOOL: THE RACE

Greetings from high school. No matter how ready and set you're feeling about starting the high school race — and believe us, it's a race, with all the frustrations and thrills one associates with marathons — you have to be feeling at least a little bit scared. Hyper, too. After all, you have many, many laps ahead of you and you've been warned that they can be, well, challenging. Your coaches on the sidelines are looking forward to guiding your progress. And your fan club (your parents, grandparents, brothers and sisters, aunts and uncles, and on and on) are anxiously awaiting the results. But when you get to the starting line, you're essentially on your own. Lots of people will give you encouragement and advice, but no one can run the race for you.

High school. It's the greatest and the toughest time of your life. We know. All of us have experienced it. And each of us is chock full of info

4

and insight based on those experiences. We've all successfully run the race and now we're remembering it, as armchair commentators. Think of this book as your newest adviser and friend, or as a group of several thousand "knowing" new pals. We've been there — and we'll be there for you.

HOW THIS BOOK CAME ABOUT

Actually, only one of us, the main author, has been out of high school for any number of years. As we begin this book, David is a freshman at Colgate University; Dale is a senior at The Calhoun School in New York City; Amanda is in her last year at the Garden City (Long Island, New York) Middle School; Ashley is a junior at Episcopal High School (Belaire, Texas); and Caroline is a freshman at The Spence School (New York, New York). And, in the course of developing, compiling, and writing this book, we've met face-to-face with more than 500 high school students from about thirty states. Throughout this book you'll find advice from teenagers from all over the country. These students, members of our National High School Reporter™ network, advise and counsel . . . and corroborate the truth and consequences of high school. They know that — more than just preparation for life — high school is a state of mind.

We started by writing letters to friends and to friends of friends in which we enclosed a four-page questionnaire. In the letters, David took a stab at explaining what this book would be about. He wrote, "This book will be the one place where you'll get the kind of honest answers to questions you want to ask but are afraid to for fear of seeming 'dorky.'" Sure, some of the stuff we've written might seem dorky to you, but bear with us. We polled thousands of high school students to find out what they wish they had known before they began their own high school races. This book answers their questions — and yours.

You'll notice that forty-five or so teenagers are quoted heavily throughout the book. These are the student delegates we selected to participate in the first annual National Teenage Summit weekend in New York City. We met for two days, discussed this manuscript, and swapped stories about high school.

The most important thing all the students we spoke with say they have learned about high school is that it is more than just forty-eight months of getting prepared for the next step (college, a job, the military . . .). It's a place and time in which everything is possible.

What follows is honest chat about high school — about what you can expect in the classroom, after school, on the home front, even in the world. This book isn't a bible; it's a primer, a how-to guide to what's what during the all-important high school years. And think about this: In just a couple of years, you'll be a reference source that junior high kids will wish they could approach to ask their "dorky" questions.

So pop yourself some popcorn, grab a soda, curl up, and start getting psyched about the next four years. After all, as Rachel Smith, an eighth grader at Rupert A. Nock Middle School in Newburyport, Massachusetts, says, "High school is truly awesome." And *Greetings from High School* is the perfect preparation for what lies ahead.

If you wish to be considered for future High School Reporter™ programs, write to us. Tell us something about how you're managing the high school juggling act.

Marian Salzman
The Bedford Kent Group
156 Fifth Avenue
8th Floor
New York, NY 10010

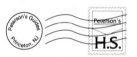

Be sure to include your name, address, telephone number, the name of your school, and the grade you're in. Tell us your favorite subjects and your most important extracurricular activities. We're looking for more reporters in grades six through twelve, and we welcome letters from American teenagers living abroad, as well as from students from all fifty states.

Author's Note: Throughout this manuscript, wherever you see a name followed by an asterisk (such as Adam* or Alicia*), the contributor's identity has been changed at his or her request. Sometimes a few identifying details have also been altered, always to protect their desire not to be named.

Greetings from High School

"High school is a challenge. Once in a while I just don't have the time to squeeze everything in, but most times I do."

Chrissa Klein, a tenth grader at Amity Regional Senior High School in Woodbridge, Connecticut

High school is a state of mind. We'll start out by introducing a few of our twelfth-grade co-authors, who will talk about their years in high school . . . now that they're drawing to a close. We hope that in reading this you'll get the same chills we feel when we hear songs like "Those Were the Days to Remember" by Billy Joel and look back on those wacky and wonderful days when we were young enough to get away with just about anything, but old enough to pull off acting like adults when we felt like it.

For some of you, high school may be just a stepping stone to what lies ahead: college. For others, it might mark the end of your formal education; it will be the school to which you refer when you turn to your kids someday and say, "When I was in school . . ." But whatever high school means to you, no matter how much you may gripe and complain now, believe us, someday . . . someday . . . .

Emily Miller of Incline Village, Nevada, a senior at Squaw Valley Academy in Olympic Valley, California:

I remember my first day in high school like it was yesterday. I was so nervous. I kept getting lost, and I was late to like every single one of my classes. And I was really nervous about all of the upperclassmen — I remember thinking that they were so intimidating. As it turned out, I had several juniors and seniors in some of my classes, so I overcame that feeling pretty quickly and learned not to get uptight around them. All of the freshmen kept hearing horror stories about "freshman initiation," but no one ever bothered us in that way.

My freshman year was really productive. I had great teachers who really inspired me to learn. One English teacher, in particular, really helped my writing skills a lot, and I still appreciate that to this day. I dated a senior, so I was pretty involved with the upperclassman "scene."

As a sophomore, I started getting more serious about my classes, but for some reason my classes seemed much easier than they had been freshman year. My teachers definitely weren't as demanding. But I knew that I was going to be in for it when the notorious junior year rolled around, so I kind of enjoyed it. And I was spending a ton of time skiing, so my social life wasn't that great.

After my junior year, I switched from public school to a tiny private school with about forty-two kids in it. It was a really big change — the classes were so much smaller, and I missed the social life of a public school. But my new school has been much more lenient in terms of letting me take off to ski in national races, and they're much more flexible about working with me for both my skiing career and my education.

Overall, I think one of the best experiences of my high school years was playing the French horn in our state's honor band with kids from all over the state. I found it really rewarding and inspiring to be playing alongside kids who were such dedicated musicians, who were so focused, and who cared so much about music. And I think I've changed a lot over these four years — I'm much more mature and independent. Through my skiing I've been alone on the road a lot, away from my family, cooking my own meals and stuff.

I think the best part about high school is that it's the only time in our lives when we're going to have so much energy and desire. There are no limits to anything for us. We have the time to develop any interests we may have, to experiment with different things, to not be tied down to one job or one social life or one relationship. Basically, we're at an age when we can do whatever makes us feel good.

Dale Allsopp of Brooklyn, New York, a senior at The Calhoun School in New York City:

In ninth grade I was really fearful of exposing my weaknesses. I wasn't able to open up or be sentimental. That has changed a lot over my high school years, and I feel like a much better and happier person. I've learned a lot about myself through teaching a class of ninth graders through a program called Peer Leadership. I give them advice about what they're going through based on my experiences, and I've gotten a great sense of fulfillment out of that.

I transferred into Calhoun, a private school, from a public school in Brooklyn, where I had developed terrible study habits. The schoolwork was so easy there that I could get away with doing absolutely nothing. Smart kids can really easily slip through the cracks at some schools, but thank God someone there realized that I was academically capable, and I was contacted by a program called Prep for Prep, where I started taking classes and which eventually helped me to find my way to Calhoun.

On my first day at Calhoun, I remember being shocked and fearful because there were very few other minority students there. It was real culture shock for me, but I told myself that I wouldn't let it intimidate me. So right from the start, I started making friends, and I've developed some friendships that I know I'll always maintain.

The most distinct change I've undergone as a result of my high school experience is that I'm really in touch with my feelings and I'm not embarrassed to express them to anyone. To me, that's been a really important part of my maturing process. My friends and teachers have really helped me a lot in that area. As a matter of fact, I wake up in the morning and actually look forward to going to school because of the people around me. I try to maintain a positive attitude; as a matter of fact, I'm never negative. Another big perk in high school is being in sports. I play basketball, and one of the biggest highs of my life was last year when we won our league championship over a team that no one expected us to challenge. I really enjoy the competitive nature of sports, as well as the friendships I've made.

Ron Palmon of Tenafly, New Jersey, a senior at Tenafly High School:

The only thing I remember about the beginning of high school was that I was running around like a madman, searching for my classes. At one point I found a panic-stricken friend who was in the same predicament, and it turned out that we were both looking for the same classroom. That calmed my nerves a little bit. I remember thinking that the school looked really

9

weird — the lockers were huge and had these locks on them that looked like there would be no way I'd ever manage to get them open.

Now that I look back on it, things progressed pretty slowly for me in high school. It wasn't like there was a huge change all of a sudden. Gradually, I became less nervous with the older kids as I began to realize that they were no different from the freshmen. But at the same time, I was very aware of where my "place" was — physically, socially, and academically.

But there was one experience that kind of jolted me into figuring out where my niche was. I took part in a theater production my junior year, an event that, I think, sort of prompted me to find what my place really was. Before that I had been an athlete — in both fall and spring sports — and I was on the "jock track." Once I realized certain things about myself, I made a conscious decision to quit the teams. But I don't think radical changes like that are uncommon in high school students. If you were to ask any of my friends whether they've noticed any changes in themselves since the time they were freshmen, every one of them would say they've changed dramatically. I look back on some of the values I had back then and I can't believe it.

Other than the natural maturing process that occurs from the time you're fourteen to the time you're seventeen, I think I've really grown up as a result of people with whom I've come into contact, classes I've taken, experiences I've had. One example is a biology teacher I had for an Advanced Placement class who was really inspiring, so much so that I'm now applying to premed programs. Another class I had, a very intense history class, required much of the outside work to be done in groups. And I think that that teamwork and the sense of accomplishment helped me to see things differently. I learned that groups of people can be real survival tools.

In high school you have the opportunity to do things you might never have the time to do again, like being in plays or participating in sports. I think that even if you're planning to go to college, where opportunities like that exist, you're going to be so much more career-oriented, and there just won't be as much time to enjoy the outside activities. That's a really important thing to keep in mind.

Alex Quintero of Miami, Florida, a senior at Christopher Columbus High School in Miami:

High school was weird at the beginning. My freshman year was the hardest in all aspects. I remember feeling really young, dorky, and unconfident. I was faced with making new friends, being in a new school, having new teachers, etc. I was really scared — I had heard rumors that the teachers were going to beat the kids up (of course, in the four years since I've been here that's never happened). But by the time sophomore year rolled around, I was much more confident. I fit in socially, and I had friends who had cars, so my social life started to get better. I also did much better in school.

Junior year was the hardest academically, by far. I had a really heavy workload in school, but it was good because I learned how to juggle things. I got a car, and my social life kept getting better and better. And now that I'm a senior, things are completely different. I feel as though I haven't picked up a book all semester long, but I'm doing really well anyway. On nights and weekends, it's not a question of "Am I going out," it's a question of "Where?" Even with college applications looming over my head, I'm still having a great time.

Over the four years in high school, my friends have become number one in my life. In junior high school, I was still pretty much dependent on my parents, but that's changed a lot. My friendships have had the greatest influence in my life over the course of high school. I don't really think kids realize how great high school can be when they're going through it, because you never really notice things until they're gone. But I do know that I'm really going to miss the freedom I have now to do what I want, when I want.

hs adviser

What's the Greatest Thing About High School?

"The freedom. I drive, I'm trusted with more responsibility, and I've got more leeway to make my own decisions." —Meredyth Cohn, North Miami Beach Senior High School, North Miami Beach, Florida

"The variety: The different people I've come into contact with and the different classes I've had." —Meraiah Foley, Oregon Episcopal School, Portland, Oregon

"The different ethnic crowds. Everyone is different, but they all come together in the same school." —Toi Jones, Martin Luther King Jr. High School, New York, New York

"The terrific friends I've made." —Lawrence Thaler, Columbia Preparatory School, New York, New York

"Making honor roll, playing basketball, keeping the friends I had and making new friends." —Dana Wolf, Hebrew Academy of the Five Towns and Rockaway, Cedarhurst, New York

"The amount of freedom I have as opposed to what I had in junior high." —Alieda Hempstead, The Spence School, New York, New York

"Making great friends and establishing good relationships with teachers." —Ryan Nelson, Newton South High School, Newton Center, Massachusetts

"So far it's been all the attention that we freshmen get from upperclassmen. Everyone is looking out for us." —Doug Heyman, Collegiate School, New York, New York

"Turning sixteen and getting my license. Having that freedom and having my parents become more lenient." —Bryan Thanner, McDonogh School, Owings Mills, Maryland

Ten Tips on How to Survive High School

☆Recognize that high school is a state of mind and do what you can to get yourself as psyched up as possible about making the most of the time and place. (Translation: Don't become a head case; don't stress out; and chill out if you need to.)

☆Don't become so focused on what other people are thinking about you that you forget that you're a good person. Similarly, be sure that at least once a day you assess your actions and reactions and decide whether you're being the person you want to be.

☆*Carpe diem.* Live for the day. Enjoy your pets, your grandparents, a walk in the park, a milkshake at the mall. Take time to find peace and don't make every day an extension of yesterday's stress.

☆Study hard, but give yourself the freedom to learn for the sake of learning. You're in school to learn, not just to get grades to please your parents, your teachers, and college admission committees or potential employers. Start reading outside of class, even if it's just popular magazines.

☆Find a foreign country that fascinates you and research it to death. Get a pen pal in that country, start exchanging information, and begin to plan a trip there so that you can see firsthand that the world is one global village.

☆Get a part-time job and try to save $20 a week or more. If you save $2,000 over a year or two, that international trip is possible.

☆Volunteer. Figure out some way to make a difference in your community and devote a couple of hours a week to the cause. Not only will you feel good and do well, you'll also meet new people and make new friends.

☆Keep a journal or at least a book of high school mementos. Before you know it, high school memorabilia will be your walk down a lane of memories of the best times of your life.

☆Get to know your family as real people. Interview them about what life was like when they were growing up; record or videotape their stories so that you have a family history that you can take with you when you plunge into the real world.

☆Develop friendships with people of all different ages. Find people who fascinate you or whom you find kind and interesting and make an effort to spend time with them. Extend yourself. P

Choosing the Right High School

**"The best thing about my high school is its size.
It is the second largest in the state. I get to meet so many
new people, and we have real quality teachers."**

Justin Bushard, a twelfth grader at Coon Rapids Senior
High School in Coon Rapids, Minnesota

Q & A: ASSESSING DIFFERENT TYPES OF HIGH SCHOOLS

**I attend the public high school in my neighborhood and don't think
I'm getting a lot out of it. How can I get the education I want
without transferring to a private school?**

Sometimes students don't even consider going to a high school other than
the one their junior high filters into — the one that their siblings, and in
some cases even their parents, attended. But a fair number of college students we've talked with tell us that once they got to college they realized
what a joke their high school experience had been academically. And,
face it, it's not just that they're looking for an excuse for why they don't
know who won the Civil War, what city is the capital of Kenya, or how
moles relate to chemistry. A lot of schools across the country are in pretty

bad shape. And it can be disconcerting to get to college and find that your classmates who went to small, private high schools have read about a hundred more classic works than you have and know every last detail of the Russian Revolution.

The fact that you're dissatisfied with your high school's academic program indicates that you probably have the intellectual curiosity and motivation necessary to offset your school's disadvantages. The first step you should take is to approach your guidance counselor or a favorite teacher and ask what you can do to move beyond the regular curriculum. Your high school may have an arrangement with another school whereby you can take classes there that are not available at your school. Your counselor or teacher can also help you put together a program of outside readings or independent studies. Another option is to supplement your courseload with a class or two at a local community college. Talk to your counselor about whether you can substitute some of these more advanced classes for those at your own school. What it boils down to is that if you really want to learn, nothing can stop you.

Does deciding to go to a vocational high school mean that colleges won't accept me because they have admission requirements I'll be unable to fulfill?

Vocational high school doesn't preclude college. Dolores Bentivegna, a guidance counselor at the Bergen County Vocational-Technical High School in Hackensack, New Jersey, tells us that, on average, nearly 20 percent of her students go on to college. (In comparison, at the local comprehensive high school, Hackensack High, nearly 40 percent of all graduates attend four-year colleges, and another 20 percent attend two-year colleges.) Entering students at Bergen Tech are required to declare a concentration and to indicate whether they are planning to continue their education at the college level. If so, guidance counselors will assist the students in planning curricula based upon that goal. "If the student knows from the beginning that he's going to college, he'll have no problem as far as credits and requirements go when the time comes to apply," says Dolores Bentivegna.

Vocational students who decide at a later point in high school to go on to college may find it difficult to fulfill all of the necessary requirements. Dolores Bentivegna says that in a case such as this, she would advise the student to take courses at a community college in order to meet all of the prerequisites of the school of his or her choice.

Students choose to attend vocational high schools for many different reasons. Often they feel that a technical skill will make them more competitive in the post–high school job market. It's wrong to assume that a vocational education will pigeonhole you into a dead-end job. Professionals such as engineers and architects are often technical school graduates. So don't write vocational school off as a place for kids who can't cut it academically. It can be an invaluable training ground for teens who hope to pursue certain technical careers.

Sometimes the idea of boarding school sounds too good to be true. What kinds of people are happiest at that sort of school?

First of all, every boarding school is different, so there's no point in generalizing. (In case you don't know exactly what a boarding school is, here's a quick definition: Boarding schools are high schools where some percentage of the students, usually a majority, sleep on campus, in dormitories, at least five nights a week. Nearly all boarding schools, though, offer seven-nights-a-week accommodations.) While one student we know is thrilled with the challenging academic and sports programs he's found at The Northfield Mount Hermon School in Northfield, Massachusetts, he admits that he ended up there because he was rejected by his first-choice school, Deerfield Academy, also in Massachusetts. Brett,* a senior from Youngstown, Ohio, says, "As an eighth grader I didn't have a lot of insight into what a school had to offer — or into what I actually expected from my high school. My advice to kids considering going away to school is to depend on a lot of input from students who are already attending boarding schools that sound interesting. And be sure that you and your parents research thoroughly what life is like at schools that seem appropriate. Find out about the dorms, the food, and the teachers. Look into the college counseling program and the extracurricular activities that the school promotes."

N E W S F L A S H

What do Presidents George Bush and John F. Kennedy, actress Sigourney Weaver, composer Stephen Sondheim, entertainer and entrepreneur Jane Fonda, and poet T. S. Eliot have in common? They're all boarding school graduates. (Source: National Association of Independent Schools)

According to a spokesperson for the National Association of Independent Schools (NAIS), "Students come to boarding school from varied economic backgrounds. They seek a boarding experience for any number of reasons: Their current day school is unable to meet their needs; they have a special talent that will be nourished by a particular boarding program; they value the close-knit community life found at boarding school; they want the structure offered by twenty-four-hour living and learning." For a free guidebook about boarding school, write to NAIS, 75 Federal Street, Boston, MA 02110-9607.

Most students who've reported unhappiness with boarding school are students who took emotional baggage to school with them or who've had to weather some heavy-duty disappointments while they've been on their own. "I don't think that my experience is completely normal," says Jane,* a sophomore at The Asheville School in Asheville, North Carolina. "Two weeks after I arrived here, my mother called to tell me that my parents were going to be divorced. While the news was not completely surprising, it was tough for me to get adjusted to a new school while dealing with the fact that I wouldn't have the same old family to head home to at vacation time." Jane adds, "My new friends have been very supportive, and I have closer friends here than I did back home in McLean, Virginia. Still, I wish that I had been there for my mom, because she's had a rocky time since Dad moved out. This year I have to get used to the idea of a stepmother."

If I go to a public high school, is a postgraduate year at a boarding school a good way to enhance my chances of getting into college?

Many college counselors encourage high school seniors who need more preparation before college to apply for a postgraduate, or thirteenth, year at one of the better-known boarding schools. Mary Lou Kelly, a guidance counselor at Wilton High School in Wilton, Connecticut, says, "Whether to pursue a PG year is an individual decision, and one that is entirely a question of the particular student's abilities and aspirations. If a student has underachieved in high school and is only beginning to prove his or her potential by the first semester of senior year, he or she should consider the extra year as an opportunity to retake the SAT and improve his or her overall record." Kelly adds that before taking this step, students should consider how strong their high school curriculum has been. If the material to be covered at boarding school would be redundant, she says, your best bet would be to attend the best possible college to which you're admitted. Once there, you should work to achieve a good record and then transfer after one or two years.

What are the pros and cons of attending a single-sex high school?

Most of the teens we've talked with who go to single-sex schools say that they feel less pressure when they don't have to deal with members of the opposite sex in the classroom. And everyone we've spoken with agrees that it's nice not to have to worry — too much — about what they look like every morning.

"I feel much more comfortable in a school that's all girls," says Alexandra Meckel, a ninth grader at The Spence School in New York City. Alexandra Marrufo, a senior at the Convent of the Sacred Heart, also in New York City, says that one of the best things about attending her school is that she's not intimidated to show her intelligence, since there aren't guys in her classrooms. Also, she says, "You don't have to deal with the tension that can exist after a breakup with a boyfriend. You won't find yourself having to sit next to each other in a classroom the next day." Doug Heyman, a ninth grader at Collegiate School in New York City, says that he enjoys the friendships he has established in an all-male setting and the ways that guys can relate to one another when there are no girls around. He adds, "Girls can be distracting in the classroom."

On the downside, many students who attend all-boys or all-girls high schools complain about the lack of opportunity to build everyday relationships with members of the opposite sex. "I'm having a harder time socializing with boys," says Alexandra Meckel. Her classmate Caroline Portny says, "We see guys at dances and parties, but it's not as comfortable as it would be if we saw them every day in more normal settings." A frequent complaint is that guys and girls tend to act "giddy" around each other when they get together on weekends, simply as a result of not being together that much during the week. And Doug Heyman says that boys in his school are extremely competitive with one another, a problem he thinks would be lessened by the presence of girls. Maria Rosel, a senior at Paramus Catholic Girls High School in Paramus, New Jersey, complains that she and her schoolmates miss out on hearing the male perspective on various things. "I think it would be really nice to get a guy's point of view on certain issues that are discussed in the classroom," she says.

In general, students we've talked with say that going to an all-girls or all-boys high school is a positive experience. Most of them don't regret having chosen a single-sex school. But, by and large, when the four years are up, they're ready to be in a coed environment.

My parents are pushing for me to go to a parochial school, but I don't consider myself very religious. How much faith must I have in order to survive at this type of school?

Most parochial schools aren't intent on ramming religion down their students' throats. Rather, their aim is to allow the students to learn more about the values, history, and beliefs of their faith. But before you commit to such a school, make sure that you and your parents thoroughly research what your daily schedule and religious requirements would be. Talk to current students, and don't be shy about asking them how they feel about the religious aspect of the school.

Zoe Schonfeld, an eleventh grader at Yeshiva of Flatbush in Brooklyn, New York, says, "Religion plays a big part of practically every minute of my day. We pray in the morning and in the afternoon, and religion is worked into my secular schedule." Although Zoe says that some of her classmates claim not to be religious, she feels that attending her school, which serves the Orthodox Jewish community, is "an incredible commitment to make, and if you're not religious, you're really not making the most of it."

On the other hand, Tara Bradley, a senior at the Convent of the Sacred Heart in New York City, says that her school doesn't require any great religious commitment, and she points out that some of her classmates are non-Catholics. "Religion at my school is more about expanding your realm of thinking than it is about learning that God said this and Jesus did that," says Tara. "It's more a matter of learning about beliefs and values and about being spiritual. Our weekly mass, the Catholic religious service, pretty much reflects what's going on in the school. It's a special time for us to think about how we're living our lives."

Public vs. Private

Students who have attended both private and public schools talk about the differences they've encountered:

Maria Rosel, Paramus Catholic Girls High School, Paramus, New Jersey:
I have attended both private and public schools and am currently a student at a private, Catholic, all-girls school. One of the biggest differences I experienced when I came to a private school was the sense of trust among myself and my classmates. I think that this comes from knowing that we're all basically from the same background. When I was in public school, I never felt the same closeness. At this school, there is a sense that my classmates and I share similar values and beliefs. Most of my classmates here have very set goals and priorities. And we receive really personalized attention from our teachers and advisers.

Ron Palmon, Tenafly High School, Tenafly, New Jersey:
I attended a private religious school for a number of years before I switched to public school, and I find that public school has been a better experience for me. At my public school we're all from the same town, so there's more of a desire to do stuff in the town. At private school, everyone was from different towns and I never felt a close sense of community. Plus, there's a little more diversity at public school.

Emily Miller, Squaw Valley Academy, Olympic Valley, California:
My public school was in a very wealthy community, and there were a lot of cliques and a lot of tension between the cliques. In private school, it's so much smaller that you can't really afford not to be friendly with everyone. This school's so small that there's no place to hide. At public school there were kids who worked really hard because they knew that they'd get out of it only what they put into it. Nothing is handed to you on a silver platter at public school.

Choosing a School: Questions to Ask Yourself

When it comes time to consider where you'll go to high school, here are some things to think about. Once you have your answers, discuss what you're thinking with your parents. And, regardless of whether it's possible for you to attend your dream school, think of ways in which you can make the most of your high school years. With your parents, formulate a game plan and set some realistic goals for the next few years.

☆In what sort of academic environment do you work best: very structured, somewhat structured, or downright casual?

☆Do you feel most comfortable in small or large classes?

☆Is it important to you that you attend a school with an ethnically/culturally/racially mixed population?

☆Are you interested in attending a boarding school? If so, how far away are you willing to go?

☆How important are sports/extracurricular activities to you?

☆Are you planning to pursue an academic or vocational course of study?

☆Do you intend to go on to college? How important is your high school's academic reputation to you?

☆What kinds of social opportunities are you looking for in high school?

☆Would you prefer a coed or single-sex environment?

☆If you're considering private school, how much is your family able and willing to spend? P

How Permanent Is This Record?

"I think that people get obsessed with their transcripts even though grades are not as important as the whole person, and the whole high school life you're leading."

Kyle Galloway, a freshman at Colgate University who graduated from Choate Rosemary Hall in Wallingford, Connecticut

Q & A: FINE-TUNING YOUR TRANSCRIPT

How can I select a program of studies that both satisfies me and prepares me for what I want in the future?

"Start off by really thinking about yourself and about what you want for the future," advises Susie Van Horn, a guidance counselor at La Porte High School in La Porte, Texas. Although many high schools have tracks (programs of study that students choose during freshman year and follow over the course of high school), you shouldn't feel locked in. "No child is poured in concrete," says Violet Ognio, a guidance counselor at Riverdale High School in Murfreesboro, Tennessee.

Choose courses that complement your strengths and challenge your weaknesses. If you find you are in over your head or are not being challenged enough once you have begun your courses, see your counselor and try to work out a different courseload.

It's okay to change your mind. No one expects you to have your life all planned out by the time you turn fifteen. But even if you're pretty sure about what you want to do, don't let that prevent you from trying lots of different things. Just because you hope to become an engineer doesn't mean you should blow off art history, for example. For all you know, you might find that that's where your talents lie. By the same token, if you're artistically inclined and wish to pursue that, don't ignore subjects like history and math. Keep an open mind about classes that you might not know too much about. College students tell us that courses that would never be required for college admission, such as typing and public speaking, have been essential to their survival in college.

Are the grades that I get in ninth and tenth grades that important overall?

Every grade you earn in high school will affect your cumulative grade point average and class standing, so your freshman and sophomore years should not be taken lightly. Don't believe the myth that junior year is the only year that counts academically, and don't forget that junior year will have its share of other time-consuming activities, such as PSATs and college planning, or career exploration for those whose next stop will be the work world.

However, if you plan to go to college and your earlier grades aren't so hot, don't panic. Numerous college students who had poor grades at the beginning of high school have told us they were able to pull their acts together in time to salvage their records and were ultimately admitted to colleges of their choice. One college freshman we spoke with is convinced that she was admitted to Williams College because she came right out in her personal interview and explained why her grades had been so bad at the beginning of high school. Her guidance counselor confirms this story but hastens to add that admissions officers at private colleges and universities have unusual freedom to look beyond the academic record. You'll find that large state universities sometimes are forced to go strictly by the numbers (GPAs and SAT, ACT, and Achievement Test scores).

What kind of extracurricular activities will look best on my record?

Experts warn against "oversubscribing" to so many activities that you — and your record — appear unfocused. Go with your gut feeling and join only those clubs, even if it's just one club, in which you have a genuine interest, rather than joining six clubs that you couldn't care less about. You will get more out of your activity and most likely will contribute more to it. Our sources tell us that college admissions officers give more weight to one leadership experience than to simple membership in five organizations.

Your choice of extracurricular activities will work most to your advantage if it reflects an academic strength or interest. For example, if your science grades are strong, complement them by starting an environmental awareness committee or by joining the science club.

Should I take on sports and other extracurricular activities even if I know that my grades might suffer?

"I am looking forward to making new friends in high school," says Matthew Thanner, a seventh grader at Ridgely Middle School in Reistertown, Maryland, "but my biggest concern is sports. I worry about making the baseball, basketball, and soccer varsity teams, and about having time to play sports and still do well in school." Lots of students entering high school worry that they won't be able to juggle academics and extracurriculars, but you shouldn't assume that your academic standing will plunge just because you delegate your time to different things. Although academics is primary, outside activities are essential — not only for a balanced high school record, but also to ease stress and help you meet other kids, teachers, and coaches. Talk to your guidance counselor prior to joining the activity and ask for advice on how to manage your balancing act. It can be done successfully — as a matter of fact, many students find that the busier they are, the more organized they have to be, so their grades often improve.

Regardless of whether you're academically oriented, be sure that you keep your grades up while you're doing your very best in home ec, in shop, or on the playing field. Even fashion models, who often postpone higher education to start working as soon as they collect their high school diplomas, recommend that you make the most of your studies, because the core curriculum in high school is sound training for life.

If I'm college bound, what is more important: my grades or the quality of my courseload?

What's most important is to strike a balance between the two. Taking an honors class that you know you can't handle or taking an easy class that you know you can ace is a waste of time. If you think you might have trouble with honors classes, talk to your guidance counselor and consider taking a less-accelerated route, not only for the grade but also to get more out of the class itself. Remember, a C is a C, visually, on your record, whether it's for an honors class or not. On the other hand, try to avoid classes that will appear to be the easy way out. Admissions officers have a keen eye for "gut" courses, and, face it, we all know that they exist out there, even in high schools with excellent reputations. Review the admissions requirements and recommendations of seven colleges and universities in this chapter's FYI section to get a feel for what kinds of classes admissions committees like to see you take.

hs adviser

AP: Is It Always an A+ Option?

Advice from Gloria Bogdanoff, guidance counselor, Lowell High School, San Francisco, California:

What are the pros and cons of Advanced Placement courses?
AP classes are extremely demanding and require a great deal of ambition and dedication. In advising a student who is considering taking AP classes, I take into account whether the student is motivated to work hard, whether he or she is an overachiever, and what the student's reasons are for wishing to take AP classes. These classes require an enormous commitment — students should expect a faster pace, more homework, and much more time required to keep up.

I strongly advise against registering for too many AP classes at once. Chances are, the student will find himself or herself overextended and in a very difficult situation. Students may be under pressure from their parents to succeed, but the parents may not be aware of the implications of AP classes. Another motivation behind pursuing AP credits often is money, as students feel that the more AP credits they receive for college, the more money they will be saving. As far as I'm concerned, this clearly indicates that the student's reasons for registering for AP classes should be reevaluated. Moreover, students should be aware that not all colleges will accept the AP credits as college credits without first issuing a placement examination during freshman orientation.

Let the Applicant Be Aware

Here's what a sample of colleges require and recommend for admission:

University of Connecticut
Storrs, Connecticut
Required: high school transcript, three years of high school math, two years of high school foreign language, SAT.
Recommended: essay, teacher recommendations.

Georgetown University
Washington, D.C.
Required: essay, high school transcript, two recommendations, interview, SAT or ACT.
Recommended: three years of high school math and science, some high school foreign language, three Achievement Tests, English Composition Test (with essay). (Test scores used for admission.)

Idaho State University
Pocatello, Idaho
Required: For non–Idaho residents, high school transcript. For Idaho residents, open admissions. (Test scores [SAT or ACT] used for counseling/placement.)

Mount Holyoke College
South Hadley, Massachusetts
Required: essay; high school transcript; three years of high school math; two recommendations; interview; SAT, three Achievement Tests, and English Composition Test.
Recommended: three years of high school science, four years of high school foreign language. (Test scores used for admission.)

University of New Mexico
Albuquerque, New Mexico
Required: high school transcript, three years of high school math and science, some high school foreign language, SAT or ACT.

North Carolina State University
Raleigh, North Carolina
Required: high school transcript, three years of high school math and science, four years of high school English, two years of high school social studies, SAT or ACT.
Recommended: essay, two years of high school foreign language, English Composition Test, Achievement Test in math.
Required of some applicants: recommendations, interview. (Preference given to state residents.)

Vanderbilt University
Nashville, Tennessee
Required: essay, high school transcript, three years of high school math, one recommendation, SAT or ACT, three Achievement Tests, English Composition Test. (Test scores used for admission and counseling/placement.)
Recommended: interview.
Required of some applicants: three years of high school science, some high school foreign language.

For more information, consult *Peterson's Guide to Four-Year Colleges* and *Peterson's Guide to Two-Year Colleges*, both published annually. P

27

Be True to Your School(work)

"When I get an A I feel really happy and excited. When I do poorly, especially in an important class, I feel upset with myself. I try to do better and ask for extra help."

Danelle Bell, an eleventh grader at Mountain Home
High School in Mountain Home, Idaho

Q & A: ACADEMIC TRUTHS AND CONSEQUENCES

Is high school that much harder than junior high?

"Expect the worst," says David Portny, a freshman at Colgate University who wishes that he had been more focused on academics during his freshman and sophomore years of high school. "At the time, it seemed like everything else was more important. In retrospect, I wish I had approached academics more seriously. I freaked junior year when I thought my grades might not get me into a 'good' college."

A lot of junior high students have told us that they're concerned about their ability to keep up with the work in high school. "I am not looking forward to the work and stress," says Rebecca Stevens, a seventh grader at The Calhoun School in New York City. "I know a lot of students in the upper school who are very stressed out about the workload. I hope that I don't end up feeling overwhelmed."

Teachers tell us that ninth-grade subjects are only slightly more demanding than eighth-grade subjects. They just seem harder because you spend so much more time on your social life and because you and your parents begin to worry about how the grades and your extracurricular record will look on college or employment applications. Victoria DeFrance, a junior at Harpeth Hall School in Nashville, Tennessee, who studies ballet six days a week, says that the toughest thing about high school is "having so much schoolwork to do and not enough time to get it all done." She adds, "The sooner you learn how to manage your time and juggle your responsibilities, the better."

And since summer reading assignments seem to be the rage throughout the country, one thing you can do to eliminate some of the stress you'll feel heading into ninth grade is to complete your summer assignments at least a few weeks before the school year begins. "If you've finished the whole summer reading list before your parents start nagging you about it, you're a whole lot better off," says David.

Besides finishing summer assignments ahead of time, what else can I do to make ninth grade easier?

The best thing you can do is get organized. Start by buying a daily organizer when you shop for school supplies. Use the organizer to record appointments, assignments, and test dates and to schedule quiet study time for subjects that require it. You can also use the organizer to schedule one-on-one time with teachers when you need extra help.

If you feel that you're starting high school with a serious academic disadvantage — you read more slowly than you'd like, you've never quite "gotten" basic algebra, or conjugating verbs in Spanish makes you gag — use the summers before and during high school to get ahead. Take a speed-reading or summer-enrichment course at a local high school. Or, if your parents want to make the investment, attend a boarding school's summer-school program. Don't shy away from confronting the "problem" subject head on. If you're looking at it simply as your least favorite subject in a roster of six, you'll probably never master it. Instead, look at it as the class on which to concentrate.

Are there certain courses that all high school students should take?

If you think you're college bound, it's important during at least the first three years of high school to take five core courses: English, math, science, history/social studies, and a foreign language. Some high schools encourage you to take a sixth course that is an offshoot of one of the others: for example, journalism, computer science, astronomy, or a second foreign language. Meet with a guidance counselor early in the year if you have questions about whether you've planned too heavy a schedule. But, at the same time, don't make school too easy by opting for only four core courses. That lack of effort is not what potential employers and colleges want to see.

Jessica Berkeley, an eleventh grader at Crystal Springs Uplands School in Hillsborough, California, says she loves French and European history and is especially interested in international relations, but she has to force herself to stick with math and science. She says, "Sometimes I wish that I didn't have to take math or science, but I understand the importance of learning all the basics in high school. Still, I can't wait to get to college, where I'll have more say over what classes I take and in what order."

Will a vocational program help me to get a job?

Many high school graduates have obtained jobs as a direct result of their high school vocational training, which is designed specifically for those who intend to seek employment directly after receiving their high school diplomas. Often students are hired by the organizations that gave them on-the-job training during their high school years.

However, if you're planning to enter a highly technical field, you may find that you'll need to pursue additional training after high school before you can be employed. Experts in fields such as computers, heating/air conditioning/refrigeration, cosmetology, and electronics more often than not have completed programs beyond the high school vocational-technical programs. So, depending on your career goals, a high school vo-tech program may or may not prepare you fully to get a job in the field.

Vocational programs will, however, provide you with more than just technical training. Through your work experiences and membership in clubs, you will be given the opportunity to hone your leadership and organizational abilities. If you know from the start of high school that you're not college bound, a vo-tech program is clearly one of your best bets.

What should I do if I really dislike a teacher I've been assigned?

First of all, don't expect to like all of your teachers. It just won't happen.

But, if you get stuck with a teacher with whom you've already had an unproductive or unpleasant experience, schedule a meeting with your guidance counselor or school head — as soon as possible. If your parents are supportive of your plan to request a switch, ask them to come along. And plan what you're going to say. No one wants to hear you moan about past injustices or the teacher's reputation as a tough guy (or flake, or whatever else he or she has been labeled). Rather, tell them exactly what you want to do. Do you want to transfer to another teacher's section? Complete the course in summer school under a different instructor? Whatever your plan, let them know you've thought it through. If nothing else works, ask the school head or your counselor or even your parents to convince the teacher to reconsider what he or she is thinking about you. Then, it's up to you to enter the class with the right attitude.

Meraiah Foley, a tenth grader at Oregon Episcopal School in Portland, Oregon, says, "The worst thing you can do is to allow the situation to become so difficult that other teachers assume that it's your fault, that you must have been disruptive or uncooperative. Still, don't back down if you know that things aren't going well; they're unlikely to get better just because you want them to. It's going to take some hard conversations at the very least."

How much does one C (or D or F) matter?

No one grade will ruin the rest of your life, but colleges and employers become concerned when they detect a pattern of mediocre performance. As a matter of fact, this author (Marian) didn't fare well in math or science throughout her high school career and still was accepted at Brown University, Georgetown University, and The Johns Hopkins University. But a pattern of "average" performances does tend to rule out extraordinary schools. The other problem with earning low grades is that you begin to settle for them instead of trying your hardest. At the beginning of each school year, set your sights on earning top grades and plot a course so that you can realize this goal.

Think of grades the way you might think about skiing down a mountain. You wouldn't get far if you abandoned your skis and poles just because you kept falling. Similarly, writing off biology because you're having trouble with some of the material is a cop-out. Keep studying and you'll get it eventually. Don't let the teacher off the hook. If you need extra help, demand it. That's his or her job, and yours, too.

How can I establish a good reputation as a student and still be popular? (Translation: Is it possible to be a brain without being a dork?)

Just because you care about getting good grades, and about learning, doesn't mean you're a one-dimensional geek. The problem is that your classmates may assume you're a brain and a cutthroat if you're super-intense about schoolwork at the expense of sports or other extracurricular activities.

Andrew Hunter of Piedmont, California, a ninth grader at Groton School in Groton, Massachusetts, says that while he loves math and science, he also recognizes the importance of being a regular guy. He hangs out in the dorms, studies with a group, plays sports, and acts low-key, even though he wants to go to an Ivy League college ("probably Harvard") or the Massachusetts Institute of Technology, and then on to medical school. One easy thing you can do to avoid being labeled a "dork" is to volunteer to help out other people by sharing your notes, by studying for tests with a group, and by taking the time to explain concepts other people haven't mastered as quickly. But avoid falling into the "knowledge is power" trap: Don't lord your academic abilities over classmates. Low-key is better, especially when you're the new kid on the block, as all freshmen are.

hs adviser

High School Is for Jugglers

According to Norm Reidel, chairman of the college and career counseling department at New Trier Township High School in Winnetka, Illinois, the ability to implement your own method of time management is the key to juggling both academics and extracurricular activities: "Students shouldn't feel that they have to sacrifice the good things in life in order to perform well in school — free time and extracurricular activities are essential to a well-rounded high school career."

Elizabeth Jewell, also a guidance counselor at New Trier Township High School, advises students who are involved with sports, theater, or other time-consuming after-school activities to maximize their free time during the day in resource rooms or study halls: "That way, after-school hours are less hectic. I strongly urge my students to chart a monthly calendar that lists the due date of every assignment, including tests, as well as all activities [such as athletic practices and games, a pep rally, etc.]. This way, students are aware, well in advance, of extra-busy times, and they can prepare a plan for how they'll squeeze everything in."

When faced with a student who is actively involved in an extracurricular activity and who is having difficulty with schoolwork, Jewell claims that she rarely, if ever, advises the student to drop the activity: "To discontinue team sports, student government, or theater group is a last-resort measure. More often than not, developing a detailed study schedule, personally suited to the student, will alleviate his or her academic difficulties."

Making the Most of Your Study Time

☆Don't procrastinate! Develop a study schedule that is both challenging and realistic, factoring in free time for munching out, relaxing, taking an occasional telephone call, and other rewards. Time management is the key to successful studying.

☆Set aside a place in which you feel comfortable — but not *too* comfortable — and use that place exclusively for studying. Consistent surroundings will lessen distractions and make it easier to concentrate.

☆If you are studying directly after school, allow yourself some time to relax before you hit the books. Have a refreshing snack to perk yourself up. Avoid sweet snacks, though, especially candy, since crashing after a fifteen-minute chocolate high won't help matters.

☆Begin by studying the most challenging (that is, the hardest) material first. Your alertness at the beginning of the study session will allow you to retain more of what's important.

☆Limit your reading sessions to about fifty minutes apiece, with twenty minutes set aside for memorization. If you own your textbooks, highlight important passages for quick and easy review.

☆If you have more than one subject to study, switch from one to another at designated intervals. Too much time spent on one subject will cause you to hit a plateau much faster, and all of the information you are trying to absorb will start to sound the same. (But don't skip around so much that you never quite get into the material.)

☆Take a ten-minute break every hour. Don't think that a few minutes of free time are going to ruin your chances of getting that A or B. You'll end up burning yourself out and regretting it.

☆If you are tempted to pull an all-nighter, don't comfort yourself with the thought of rewarding yourself the next day. You still have to take the exam, go to other classes, and be on top of things.

☆Joining a study group can be to your advantage, but only if you already have a base knowledge of the material. Don't get together with friends, thinking that you'll learn everything from them — they might be thinking the same thing. If you know all the material, going over certain key elements can be helpful; many times we remember things better after we've discussed them with others. P

5

Teacher's Pet

"The teachers at my school are well qualified and seem to be able to communicate well. Most important, they are very caring and fair."

Julie Weiss, an eleventh grader at Springbrook
High School in Silver Spring, Maryland

Q & A: TEACHER-STUDENT RELATIONS

What can I do to get my teachers to like me without all the other kids thinking I'm a brownnose?

Somehow, common courtesies — such as looking people in the eye and listening to them when they speak — seem to get put on the back burner when it comes to dealing with teachers. Human nature dictates that we like others to respect us and not to treat us rudely. First and foremost, teachers like students to be interested in the subjects the teachers are teaching. Acting bored is a sure way to get on your teachers' nerves. You don't have to fake a lifelong interest in the subject, just pay attention in class and ask a question once in a while. Even small gestures like getting to class on time and having your books open and ready to go will make a big difference in how your teachers perceive you.

First impressions really count, so start off the year right. Alex Quintero, a senior at Christopher Columbus High School in Miami, Florida, advises: "Once you're on a teacher's bad side, it's hard to get him to change his mind about you. Get on his good side right from the start."

Sometimes I have a choice of teachers for a particular class. What characteristics should I look for in a teacher?

"Look for genuineness, fairness, creativity, and good time-utilization in the classroom, as well as at the teacher's overall personality and the manner in which he presents himself," says William W. Cooper, a guidance counselor at Corbin High School in Corbin, Kentucky. Don't be afraid to talk to students who have had a teacher prior to you to find out what to expect. And, if you have a choice of teachers, feel free to discuss each option in confidentiality with your guidance counselor.

Some questions to ask about a potential teacher:

- How willing is he or she to spend time with students after class?
- Are the teacher's classes mostly lectures, or do they involve class participation?
- How does he or she test and grade?
- Is the teacher really interested in the subject matter he or she is teaching?
- Is the teacher in tune with the knowledge- and interest-level of students?

Everyone keeps telling me that high school teachers are really strict. What if I'm scared of or intimidated by them?

Just because they're tough in the classroom doesn't mean that teachers are out to get you. College students we've interviewed have told us that they are glad now that some of their teachers in high school were very demanding, because as a result the students were better prepared when they got to college.

But, more often than not, you'll find there's not much difference between teachers in junior high and teachers in high school. There are tougher teachers and easier teachers at every level — it all depends on the course, the teacher's personality, and his or her style of teaching.

Most of us have felt intimidated by teachers at some point or another, but remember: Teachers are there because they like kids. They like students to say hi to them in the hallways and to get to know them outside of the classroom. Developing good relationships with students is one of the most gratifying parts of a teacher's job. And keep in mind that you will be needing teacher recommendations down the road, recommendations that can make or break you.

N E W S   F L A S H

Colleges regard recommendations written by tenth-grade teachers the same way as those written by twelfth-grade teachers. Therefore, consider staying in close touch with a favorite tenth-grade teacher for the duration of high school. This way, you'll have a good friend and sounding board, and that person will be able to recommend you not only on the basis of your in-class performance but also on the progress you've made over the years on a personal level.

Is it wise to become buddies with my high school teachers?

"Student-teacher friendships are an extremely gratifying part of my job," says Celia Pineiro, a teacher at Dodge City Senior High School in Dodge City, Kansas. Most teachers we have spoken with have maintained friendships with students long after the students have graduated. However, it's a mistake to let your friendship with a teacher conflict with the professionalism that must be maintained at school. Other students may become upset if a teacher and student act like buddies in the classroom.

One caveat: Do not — repeat, do not — even consider dating a teacher. Not only is it illegal in most cases, but it also puts the teacher's job in jeopardy and can add significantly to the stress a high school student already feels. We interviewed a boarding school graduate, Jay,* who had been romantically involved with his English teacher, Lucy,* for two years. Both of them caution others against trying such an arrangement, since, in the words of Lucy, who is now twenty-six, "Neither one of us is better for having broken the taboo." Lynn,* a student at a large public high school outside Chicago, told us, "In the beginning it was thrilling for me to date my math teacher. But after a while the cover-up became draining and my parents eventually caught us and freaked. Even though they liked Dave* on some levels, they were very angry that he was dating their sixteen-year-old daughter. By the beginning of senior year they persuaded me to break it off, and I have. But it's tough to walk past Dave and not have regrets, even though I know that my parents' advice was right."

hs adviser

How to Make Your Teacher Your Friend

Here's what some recent high school graduates have to say about befriending teachers:

"I just treated my teachers as my peers . . . and it also helped to be a good student in the classroom and to really listen to what they had to say." —Janice Moore, Louisiana State University (Mount Carmel Academy, New Orleans, Louisiana)

"I really liked a number of teachers I had in high school. Once I got to know the teacher as a person, it became easier for me to respect his or her commitment to the subject matter. I wish that I had made even more of an effort to find out what motivated those teachers I respected but never made time to know well." —Kyle Galloway, Colgate University (Choate Rosemary Hall, Wallingford, Connecticut)

"I got to know my teachers through activities like theater. That way, I knew they had similar interests to mine, which is a solid foundation for a friendship." —Vince Princiotta, Lafayette College (Byram Hills High School, Armonk, New York)

"I wasn't afraid or intimidated to ask questions or to go to them with problems, even if they were personal. It made them feel good to be able to help, and they really got to know me. I had a lot of my teachers for more than one year, and I was also involved in cheerleading, so I think that my teachers were more receptive in that they knew I was very busy and involved in our school. In high school I always treated my teachers with respect because there seemed to be such an age gap between us." —Cindy Fazio, New York University (Riverdale High School, Murfreesboro, Tennessee)

Getting on Their Good Sides

The following are some responses of high school teachers when asked, "What would you tell students who want to know how to get along better with teachers in the classroom?"

"The most important thing is to listen. Even if the student is shy and doesn't like to speak up, I can tell if he or she is listening, and it makes a big difference." —Alan Bradshaw, Mesa High School, Mesa, Arizona

"Be willing to learn, communicate, and tell the truth. Be open." —Richard Esler, Wasatch Academy, Mount Pleasant, Utah

"Honesty plays a major part. If you don't get your assignment done, be truthful about it. You're worse off if you lie, because the teacher always knows it." —Barb Bickel, Bowman High School, Bowman, North Dakota

"Let the teacher know that you have an open mind and no preconceptions about the subject . . . that maybe you can learn something from this class. There's nothing worse than a student with an attitude like, What a drag, I have to take this class." —Rico Hernandez, Ph.D., Chaminade College Prep, West Hills, California

"Students should at least attempt all of the assignments. Even if they have trouble with the subject matter, I always know whether or not they gave it a shot." —Peter Frank, Chatfield Senior High School, Littleton, Colorado

"Knowing that the student is at least putting forth the effort makes me willing to spend extra time with him or her." —Tina Cliff, Brookstone School, Columbus, Georgia

"Act enthusiastic and happy to be in the classroom. Look at the teacher, smile, and make direct eye contact." —Linda Hardy, John Dickinson High School, Wilmington, Delaware

"Mutual respect is key. Always show common courtesy to the teacher by doing quality work." —Samia Ferraro, Martin County High School, Stuart, Florida

"Students need to be prepared for class. If they do their homework and they're prepared, they'll be more confident." —John Niles, Groton School, Groton, Massachusetts P

39

The Guidance System

"My guidance counselor helps me a lot with course selection. Overall, guidance counselors are very helpful."

Victor Jones, an eleventh grader at Callaway
High School in Jackson, Mississippi

Q & A: MAKING THE MOST OF YOUR GUIDANCE COUNSELOR

What can my guidance counselor do for me?

Many students are convinced that guidance counselors serve only one purpose: to help kids apply to college. The truth is, your guidance counselor can help you out in a number of ways, from junior high on, even if you're not planning to go to college. Guidance counselors monitor your progress and the number of credits you've earned. They make sure you don't find yourself unable to graduate with your class someday because you forgot to take that home economics requirement you never knew about.

Depending on your school, your guidance office also may offer seminars (some of which are open to parents) on topics ranging from problem solving to test taking. Don't wait until you're panicked about some standardized test to take advantage of these sessions. They can really give you an edge. Your guidance counselor also can act as a mediator between you and your teacher or even the school administration should any problems arise.

Most important, your guidance counselor is there to give you advice. Whether it be a problem with a classmate or a scheduling conflict, your counselor can help you figure out what to do. Look to your counselor as a mentor, someone who can guide you over the rough spots.

When should I start seeing my guidance counselor on a regular basis?

Most students begin biweekly, one-on-one contact with their guidance counselors during the fall of twelfth grade. Don't consider these sessions merely a formality, a way for the school to keep track of your application process if you're college bound. Counselors act as liaisons with colleges and very often have access to inside information about various schools. They may have developed a relationship with admissions officers at some universities, and they might be willing to put in a good word for you. So don't write them off! Guidance counselors also can be a great source of information about opportunities in the military and can help steer your job-search process.

More than 60 percent of the students we surveyed report that they wanted to begin seeing their guidance counselors on a regular basis during junior year. Unfortunately, more than half of these students say that their counselors were too busy to meet regularly with them until senior year. Don't let a counselor's complaints about a busy schedule discourage you. Adam Kanner, a sophomore at North Miami Beach Senior High School in North Miami Beach, Florida, says, "If you really want advice, insist that a guidance counselor see you. Sure, they're busy, but that doesn't change the fact that you need help. Usually, if the counselor sees that you're interested and that you need help, he or she will make time to meet with you."

Alex Quintero adds, "Even before senior year, try to develop a relationship with a counselor so that you have the benefit of his or her insight when you make your final course selections and when you're developing your preliminary college admissions game plan. The better your adviser knows you, the more accurate his or her advice will be."

What can I do if I don't get along with my guidance counselor?

"My guidance counselor has no idea what I'm really like, and she makes judgments about me anyway," says Joseph,* an eighth grader from Long Island, New York. Many students feel that their guidance counselors are really behind the times and clueless about the things that concern kids today. Of course, this is just one side of the story: Many other students swear by their counselors and insist that these advisers are their strongest supporters, especially when the going gets rough.

Fred,* a high school junior from Wilmington, Delaware, told us, "When I realized that my father had a drinking problem, my guidance counselor was the person I turned to. He was there for me — and gave me great suggestions about ways to take charge of a pretty nasty situation. He ended up referring me to a support group that has helped a great deal."

If you find that your counselor isn't terribly helpful, it may be possible to switch. Ask the director of your guidance office for a reassignment, but be prepared with concrete reasons for wanting someone new. Those of you at smaller schools may find that your options are more limited. In that case, your best bet is to choose some other adult to be your unofficial counselor. Ask your favorite teacher or coach to help you out — you will benefit much more from the advice of someone whom you respect and who knows you well.

One college freshman we know cautions against telling your guidance counselor too much too soon. She says, "Take time to get to know your counselor and his or her reputation. Be sure that he or she is professional enough to have perspective on the normal passages of teenage life. I made the mistake sophomore year of confiding in my counselor about my boyfriend troubles and about the fact that my parents had recently separated. It made it that much tougher for me to go back in spring of junior year, acting like I could walk on water and insisting that I had the stellar kind of record that would make me a shoo-in to my then-first-choice college. I could feel my counselor trying to look inside me to see if I was for real. And I know that her doubts influenced how she counseled me about colleges and careers. She thought that I was flighty because I had been fairly lovesick and confused for a few months during tenth grade."

Should I consider hiring a private college adviser?

Since the college application process takes a great deal of time and energy and is most likely not going to be one of the most enjoyable experiences of your life, you might want to consider hiring a professional counselor who can ease you through the process and make it somewhat less stressful.

Independent educational consultants help students decide which schools they should apply to, arrange interviews and overnight visits, and oversee the writing of application essays. Students who go to very large high schools and suffer from a lack of direct, personalized attention can benefit greatly from these services. But professional advice costs money — lots of it. We spoke to one private counselor in San Diego, California, who charges $400 for a one-time consultation and $2,300 for ongoing consultations. If you do opt to hire a private consultant, make sure your application doesn't show it. College admissions officers can spot a prepackaged, phony application a mile away.

For leads on independent college counselors, have one of your parents check with college admissions officers to find out whom they respect and why. And beware of any potential adviser who promises you the sun, the moon, or Harvard, as no one can guarantee you admission anywhere, no matter how connected, or talented, he or she is.

How involved should my parents be with what goes on between me and my guidance counselor?

This is a touchy subject. On the one hand, guidance counselors don't like dealing with pushy parents who may not be quite realistic when it comes to their child's capacities and limitations. On the other hand, no one likes to see parents who are completely uninvolved in their child's education. What's most important is that you be comfortable with the extent of your parents' involvement. You may not want your folks to take complete control of your academic life, but there's no sense in trying to keep them out of the process entirely. After all, high school is an important time in your life, and your parents probably can — on occasion — give some good advice.

Encourage your parents to take advantage of informational sessions that most guidance offices hold to keep both students and parents up to date on all that's happening at school. How far you want to involve them beyond that will depend on you and your parents. If you feel as though you're under a magnifying glass, tell them that. Ask them to cut you some slack. If your grades are good and your behavior is reasonable, most parents will at least try to give you some breathing space.

hs adviser

Rating the Counselors

"The only time I dealt with my guidance counselor was senior year, and he was helpful in choosing colleges." —Lisa Dembiczak, Washington State University (Thomas Jefferson High School, Auburn, Washington)

"My high school gave us a training class on using our guidance office, but I didn't go to my counselor very often. I basically was forced to go to her for minor scheduling problems." —Ari Friedman, Rochester Institute of Technology (Walt Whitman High School, Bethesda, Maryland)

"The counselors at my school were very much on top of things, including what my options would have been had I decided to take a year off before college. I decided not to go to Australia at the last minute, but my college counselor would have been supportive either way." —Kyle Galloway, Colgate University (Choate Rosemary Hall, Wallingford, Connecticut)

"When it came time to be thinking about getting into college, I went to my guidance counselor. But since I went to a very large high school, I went only if I had a specific problem or question." —Brian Weinstein, Duke University (Syosset High School, Syosset, New York)

"My guidance counselor had thirty-seven years of experience and really helped me to narrow down my choices of colleges." —Bill Bush, Colby College (St. George's School, Newport, Rhode Island)

"My guidance counselor made me lose confidence in my abilities, and, as a result, I didn't apply to any 'reach' schools. He told me that I didn't have a chance at an Ivy school, but now that I look back, I wish I hadn't listened to him. I think I might have had a chance." —Barry,* Washington University (a suburban Boston high school)

A Sample of Sessions and Seminars You Can Expect Over the Next Four Years

Grade Nine: Orientation
Don't worry, no one expects you to figure out high school on your own. During the first week, you'll probably have a class assembly with counselors who will talk to you about the school and about course listings, requirements, schedules, and other matters. There might also be seminars available during study hall.

Examples of seminars for freshmen available at Rice Memorial High School, South Burlington, Vermont:

"Getting Oriented to High School"
"Your High School Record: What You Will Do and How It Will Get Recorded"
"Your Past School Record: What We Think We Know About You"
"This Year and Next: Examining What You Have Done So Far and Preparing for the Next Step"

Grade Ten: Sampler
This is a good time to sign up for individual meetings with your counselor so he or she can really get to know you.

Seminars for sophomores at Rice Memorial:
"Learning How to Learn More About Yourself"
"Learning About Life After High School"
"Continuation of the Four-Year Plan"
"Occupational Information and Career Decision-Making"

Grade Eleven: Prep
You'll continue one-on-one meetings with your counselor this year and probably will begin to concentrate on post–high school plans.

Seminars for juniors at Rice Memorial:
"Preparing for the PSAT"
"Interpretation of the PSAT"
"Involving Parents in Post–High School Planning"
"Individual Student/Parent Conferences"

Grade Twelve: Sink or Swim
You'll finally have reached the point at which you can't put off decisions any longer. If you're applying to college or into the work world, your counselor will be guiding you through the application process.

Seminars for seniors at Rice Memorial:
"Evening Meeting with Parents: Wrap-up on Post–High School Planning"
"Coordinating Financial Aid Workshop"
"Monitoring Graduation Requirements" P

Don't Stress Out

**"We stress about the workload. Math classes
at my school are really hard, and my parents
put pressure on me to do well."**

Sheryl Brodeur, a ninth grader at Memorial High School
in Manchester, New Hampshire

Q & A: SYMPTOMS AND SOLUTIONS

What is going to stress me out in high school?

Some students begin worrying about high school before they even get out
of junior high. Jeff Toohig, an eighth grader at Garden City Middle
School in Garden City, New York, says that his biggest concern about
high school is that he won't get good teachers. Jamie Stover, an eighth
grader at the Gill St. Bernard's School in Gladstone, New Jersey, says, "I
am worried that I will be overwhelmed by the workload in my high
school. But I'm looking forward to going to boarding school and to playing high school hockey." Jamie Sattel, an eighth grader at Portsmouth
Middle School in Portsmouth, Rhode Island, adds, "My biggest concerns
are the drugs, the workload, and the seniors. I don't want to have to wor-

ry about any of them. But I am looking forward to getting home earlier and to being on the hockey team. Also, I think that in high school it will be easier to have more friends."

These junior high students aren't alone. Nearly 95 percent of the 6,000 students we surveyed reported that they feel stressed out about something. Their answers to what stresses them out are less uniform, but Allison Engel, a junior at The Spence School in New York City, puts things in a nutshell. According to Allison, stress in high school is caused by "too many things to do — people pulling me in a thousand different directions and expecting me to be capable of everything."

No doubt about it, high school is stressful. Kids are under a lot of pressure these days to do well — not just at one or two things, but at virtually everything. Where's the pressure coming from? Teachers, parents, but, most of all, the students themselves. Even if you don't care about your grades or schoolwork, you'll find something to worry about: popularity, dating, peer pressure, parents, and on and on. High school can be a difficult time. But knowing how — and when — to deal with stress can make all the difference in allowing you to enjoy what can be four totally excellent years.

Students we've surveyed across the country tell us that the biggest causers of stress are:

- parents, family life, parental divorce or separation
- getting into college
- other people's shortsightedness and lack of understanding
- not having a social life
- unhappiness with personal appearance
- exams, too much academic pressure, too much homework
- lack of sleep

The consensus among many students is that stress comes and goes in cycles. Students tell us that when it's bad, it's really bad, particularly during weeks in which everything seems to be due at the same time. Jennifer Yuil, a senior at Brooks School in North Andover, Massachusetts, says that stress is caused by "too much homework or too many commitments that fall on the same week or day. There is no time to fit them all in."

Other students, particularly those who are involved in athletics or other activities, feel a constant pressure. Bryan Thanner, a junior at McDonogh School in Owings Mills, Maryland, says, "School is very demanding, academically and athletically. I *always* have something to do. As an athlete, I have very little free time." And a junior at a girls' school in New York City says that she feels constant stress because of the "pressure to keep up to the standards that I have set for myself, as well as to keep up to par with my classmates." But not all of the stress teenagers feel has to do with academics.

A sophomore at Greenwich High School in Greenwich, Connecticut, says that his parents' marriage is more stress-producing than anything else in his life. "They fight constantly and have separated twice," he says. "My brother and I wait for the day when they finally will decide to divorce. It's very rough being old enough to realize that you're one of the two reasons, my brother being the other, that two decent people are staying together and making each other miserable."

And Kathryn Alexander, an eleventh grader at Bearden High School in Knoxville, Tennessee, says that her stress is caused by the length of her commute. She spends nearly two hours commuting each day and even longer on Fridays, when, she says, "I often go back to school, or near there, for a dance or party." Even though Kathryn likes to drive, she says that the amount of time behind the wheel can really make her tense.

Is the stress going to be much worse in high school than in junior high?

"Everyone knows that high school is going to be more stressful socially than junior high," says Ron Palmon, a senior at Tenafly High School in Tenafly, New Jersey. "Just knowing that you're going to be meeting new people and that you're going to be in unfamiliar surroundings is a big pressure. Also, as you get older you're naturally going to be studying more and expecting more from yourself." But most students feel that once you've become acclimated to high school, it isn't that much tougher than junior high. "Going into high school was a whole transition, and scary at first," says North Miami Beach Senior High School sophomore Mindy Jones. "But it's really fun now, and I absolutely love it!"

Those of you who have older brothers or sisters have probably been tormented by horror stories about high school. "I hear that there are only a few minutes to get to classes — I'm worried about getting lost and being late all the time," says Rachel Smith, an eighth grader at Rupert A. Nock Middle School in Newburyport, Massachusetts. Other junior high students worry that they'll be picked on by upperclassmen and excluded from all the cool parties. One of the few junior high students we talked to who don't have this concern is Joey Schmidt, an eighth grader at the Gill St. Bernard's School in Gladstone, New Jersey. "My father is the principal, so I'm not worried about older kids picking on me," he says. "They all know me." But even without Joey's advantages, most high schoolers admit that it's really not bad once you're there. You'll figure out the new schedule and building in no time, and you'll be so busy with your own social life, you won't have time to worry about what the older kids are doing.

College freshman David Portny says, in retrospect, "There's more to life than being stressed out. I look back now on things that used to bother me and laugh. But that doesn't make it any less traumatic for ninth graders who have to face all the things I once faced."

What can I do to combat stress?

Everyone has his or her own way of dealing with stress, but firsthand advice from high school students can help you come to grips with some of the issues you're about to experience. "Even if you're in a difficult situation, just put everything into perspective by detaching yourself from it and looking at it from an outsider's point of view," advises Ron Palmon. Mindy Jones says, "Just try not to compare yourself with everyone else. Base your progress on your own standards, not on anyone else's." Lots of students say they count on parents and others to listen to their gripes and to let them vent their frustrations. Ashley Bryan, a junior at Episcopal High School in Belaire, Texas, says she depends on friends to help her chill out. "I talk on the phone a lot — vocalizing things helps me put them in perspective. I like to talk about everything from my classmates to what I did that day." When Victoria DeFrance feels anxious, she turns to her best friend, a person she describes as "someone who is always there, whom I can talk to."

Other students suggest the following stress-busters:

- be active in sports
- listen to music
- shop
- scream (in private)
- go for long walks
- write in a journal

There are lots of ways to deal with stress, and lots of people who are eager to help you through tough times. Your school social worker/psychologist, your guidance counselor, your teachers and parents, and your friends are just some of the people to whom you can turn. Talking things over with a sympathetic listener will almost always make you feel better. Here's a final word of advice from Dr. Irvin Faust, director of guidance at Garden City High School in Garden City, New York: "Just keep in mind that life is a marathon, not a sprint." In other words, don't stress out — you've got a long life ahead of you.

What exactly is depression?

Every one of us has complained of being depressed at one time or another. It's important to look at what typically causes this melancholy and at what can be done to overcome it. And it's also vital to recognize when one's depression is so serious that it's time to seek professional help.

"It's easiest to define depression in terms of how I feel when I'm low," says Mindy Jones. "*Low* is the right word for it. I feel like I'm dragging, like I have no energy, and like I am expecting something gloomy to happen." She adds, "There are some kids in school who are severely depressed a lot of the time. They just sulk, and they are so angry or upset that they're too paralyzed to make changes."

More than a quarter of all high school students report occasional depression, and some suffer so much that professional help, including counseling and antidepressants (prescription drugs), is the only remedy. Some warning signs of depression are constant crying jags, as opposed to a sniffle or two, and migraine headaches and stomach pains. But these symptoms may appear for other reasons as well, and it's important to determine whether depression is, in fact, the culprit.

Here are a couple of things to consider if you think that you're depressed:

- Can you see a solution to whatever's bothering you?
- Do you understand why you're feeling blue or what it will take to cheer yourself up?

If your answers to these questions are no, then consider the following:

- Do you regularly sleep more than eight hours a night?
- Do you sometimes think about how much easier everything would be if you were dead, or at least in a coma?

If you answer yes to these questions, try to identify the main things that are bothering you and divide the list into those problems that can be solved — "I hate my brother" or "I feel unattractive" — and those that can never be changed but that you can learn to deal with — "My dog died suddenly" or "My parents got divorced when I was five."

Once you've pinpointed the negatives in your life — or even if you're unable to determine them exactly — make an appointment with your school social worker or your family doctor. Explain that you're feeling low and that you'd like some help getting your life on track. Don't be put off by what other people might think or say about your going for help; take pride in the fact that you're sturdy enough to recognize that you need more than your family and friends can give you. (Incidentally, nearly 30 percent of the high school students we polled reported that they have consulted with a psychiatrist, a psychologist, or a social worker.) Talking things out with your peers can also be helpful. Sarah Ribbeck, an eleventh grader at Lamar High School in Houston, Texas, says that church youth group meetings are a great time to talk things over with other young people and help put things into perspective.

I think one of my friends abuses alcohol. What should I do?

According to the National Council on Alcoholism, alcohol is the number-one drug problem among America's youth. So chances are very good that you know someone in your school who abuses alcohol. If you are concerned about a friend's drinking habits, take this word of advice from Alice Petropoulos, program director, Outpatient Clinic, Pace/Parkside Recovery Center, New York City:

"Observe your friend's actions for a little while before you do anything. One isolated incident isn't grounds for concern. But if you notice a pattern, approach him or her and say, 'I want to tell you something because I care about you.' Recount your observations. Remind your friend of what he or she has done under the influence of alcohol, which he or she may not remember (e.g., blacking out or fighting). Then say to your friend, 'I'm very worried, and I wish you would talk to someone about it.'"

Petropoulos does not advise bringing a parent or another adult into the situation against your friend's wishes unless your friend is talking about suicide. The best thing to do is to take every action possible to convince your friend that he or she will benefit from talking to a professional or another concerned adult.

My school brings in these speakers who scare us about substance abuse, but I don't believe a little bit of partying is all that bad. How can we convince our parents to let us drink once in a while?

The U.S. Department of Health and Human Services has found that most alcohol- and drug-use patterns are well established by the time the user reaches age twenty-five. And though you might think that a little bit of partying isn't all that harmful, tons of statistics show that some of the results of drinking aren't harmless at all. In fact, they're pretty scary.

But you're in high school in the 1990s, and from what you've told us, a high school party without alcohol is a rare animal these days. This doesn't mean, of course, that you have to imbibe at these parties. But should you choose to do so, it's up to you to make it clear to your parents that even though you might be attending parties where alcohol is available, you're handling it responsibly. Tell them that it's important for you to know that they won't come down too hard on you if you should have to call them up for a ride some night when you've been drinking. But even if they do come down on you, you're better off getting "killed" by your parents for being drunk and needing a ride home late at night than getting really killed — or killing someone else — because you made the mistake of getting behind the wheel when you were drunk.

Here are a few things that you should be aware of:

Myth: Beer and wine have less alcohol and are less potent than hard liquor.
Fact: A 12-ounce can of beer has about the same amount of alcohol as a 5-ounce glass of wine or a 1.5-ounce shot of whiskey. A person who drinks a lot of beer is drinking a lot of alcohol. And just two drinks of any kind can seriously impair your judgment and performance.
Myth: Experimenting with alcohol and drugs is just a harmless phase that is a normal part of growing up.
Fact: Drugs and alcohol pose serious risks to the health of teenagers at an important point in their physical, emotional, social, and intellectual development. Every year, 48,000 youngsters die or are injured in drug- or alcohol-related incidents — no harmless experiment. The United States has 4.6 million teens who are problem drinkers. (Source: The American Council for Drug Education)

Here are some hotlines that can help you get answers to questions about alcohol and drugs:

Alcohol and Drug Helpline: 1-800-252-6465
Cocaine (and crack): 1-800-COCAINE and 1-800-662-HELP
"Just Say No": 1-800-258-2766

If you'd like to find out more about Al-Anon and Alateen or to find a local chapter if there isn't one listed in the Yellow Pages, write:

Al-Anon and Alateen
P.O. Box 862 Midtown Station
New York, NY 10018

You wouldn't believe how frequently some people threaten to commit suicide. What should I do when one of my friends tells me that he or she plans to end things?

Follow this advice from Thomas Caffrey, Ph.D., a clinical psychologist in New York City: "First, take it very seriously. Listen to your friend and respect what he or she is saying. You might be the only one this person has found it possible to talk to. Don't be deaf to it. Don't act as though he or she is joking, even if you think he or she might be. Respect the seriousness of the feelings that are leading your friend to have suicidal thoughts.

"Second, try to find some way to have your friend talk with some adult who might be helpful, whether it be a counselor, parent or other family member, a minister, rabbi, priest, teacher, psychologist, psychiatrist, or physician. Try to move the problem toward some adult without seeming to unload your friend from yourself. Stay with him or her in the search for the answer to the problem. Don't dismiss either your friend or his problem in any way. Stay with it until some responsible adult is located and contacted, and, even then, let him or her know that you are not 'turning your friend over' to an adult. Make your friend aware that you are still by his or her side.

"If, however, your friend is completely resistant to going to an adult, you should take it upon yourself to make sure that doesn't happen, even if it means going against his or her wishes. Your first responsibility is to keep your friend alive. Keeping your friendship comes second to that. You can't do number two if number one hasn't been accomplished."

For more information about teenage suicide or to talk about how you're feeling, call The Samaritans, a 24-hour hotline: (617) 247-0020. They do accept collect calls.

Stress-Busters

"I shop and hang out in the park or at someone's house with my friends." —Amanda Abraham, Garden City Middle School, Garden City, New York

"To me, stress isn't even an issue. High school has so much to do with social issues . . . boyfriends, friends, clothes, competition. I just block it out and, especially by senior year, relax and enjoy myself." —Tracy Herman, Lower Merion High School, Ardmore, Pennsylvania

"I like to talk out my problems with either my friends or my parents. I had some boyfriend problems and I talked to my parents about everything. It really helped a lot." —Tracy Weinberg, Lower Moreland School, Huntingdon Valley, Pennsylvania

"I take a long drive in my car with the windows down and the radio blaring. It always makes me feel a lot better." —Alex Quintero, Christopher Columbus High School, Miami, Florida

"I find ways to channel my stress into sports. Also, I make an effort just to find my own niche in the world." —Garth Svenson, Brooks School, North Andover, Massachusetts

"I like to just mellow out and be by myself, or I talk everything over with my grandmother, who knows and understands me better than anyone else." —Mindy Jones, North Miami Beach Senior High School, North Miami Beach, Florida

How Stressed Are You?

Experts say that some of the most common warning signs of stress are often so minor that they go unnoticed. If you're not feeling quite up to par, don't try to convince yourself that it's normal. Your body is trying to tell you something.

Ask yourself if you experience any of the following:

Sleeplessness: Do you have trouble falling or staying asleep? A sleepless night here and there may be pretty common, but frequent insomnia among teenagers should be checked out right away. Insomnia is one of the early warning signs of stress.

Headaches and Neck-aches: Tension headaches and neckaches can afflict you in a matter of seconds and can cause big trouble. If there's no underlying physical problem, headaches and neckaches that are frequent enough to interfere with your performance of everyday tasks most likely indicate stress.

Zits: Acne is just one of many skin problems that can be aggravated by stress. Does your skin break out right before final exams or a big date? Stress strikes again!

Sudden Weight Gain or Loss: Stress affects our eating habits in various ways. For some, stress induces bingeing. For others, it causes a loss of appetite. Try to eat as consistently as possible, minimizing between-meal snacks and not eating too much or too little of any one thing. Studies show that a healthy diet helps us to think and learn better.

Stomachaches: Stomachaches may be a direct result of your poor eating habits, but more often than not the cause is a "nervous stomach." Stress seems to hit our digestive systems in a big way and can cause severe pains and/or diarrhea.

Substance Abuse: If you rely on any form of drugs or alcohol to make it through the day — even if it's an over-the-counter medication — you may be reacting to stress. The minute you notice a dependence, see your doctor.

General "Under-the-Weather-ness": Many of us wake up virtually every morning feeling lousy, which may be why we try to convince ourselves that it's normal. But it's not! Remember when you were a little tyke? You woke up in the morning, happy as a clam. Pinpoint what it is that's causing your overall lethargy and come to grips with it before it gets the best of you. **P**

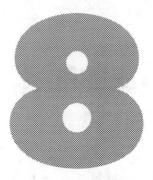

Survival Strategies for When the Going Gets Tough

"My best survival strategy is to get together with friends and make outlines. The worst thing you can do is cram. The best thing you can do is allow yourself plenty of time to study."

Lauren Cutler, a tenth grader at Cherokee High
School in Marlton, New Jersey

Q & A: THE HIGH SCHOOL JUGGLING ROUTINE

What do high school students do to handle all of the different things going on in their lives?

The hectic pace and ever-increasing pressures of the teenage years can seem overwhelming. What with schoolwork, peer pressure, drugs and alcohol, competition, fear of failure, working parents, family problems, wild-and-crazy romances, and traumatic breakups, teenagers today are required to be tougher and faster just to keep up.

How can you deal with the pressure without losing your cool? Adam Kanner says, "Every high school student feels the challenge of juggling the 'traumas' of being a teenager. The best way to deal with it is just to try to be yourself . . . but don't do that by isolating yourself or being in your own world." Tracy Herman of Ardmore, Pennsylvania, also warns against cutting yourself off from possible supporters: "Having a good group of friends really helped me through high school, because I knew that whatever I was going through at any given time, they were going through also."

If you find yourself unable to cope with everything in your life, keep in mind that you'll probably look back at high school and wonder what you possibly could have found traumatic about it. The high school years are full of pressures, but they're also full of fun and learning and excitement. "Don't blow things out of proportion," advises Tracy Weinberg, a sophomore at Lower Moreland School in Huntingdon Valley, Pennsylvania.

The power of positive thinking is remarkable when it comes to maintaining the ability to juggle your highs and your lows. Whenever you're in the dumps, make a list of the pros and cons of your life as a teenager. If you're honest with yourself, it's more than likely that you'll come out heavy on the pros. Thinking negatively, even if just for a moment, will make you feel worse and can be totally destructive. Learn to concentrate on the good things in life and appreciate them for what they are. If you need to take your mind off your troubles, read a good book or take a long walk.

And, most important, don't be afraid of failure. No matter what you and your parents seem to expect, you're not perfect and you never will be. Anne Morrow Lindbergh, noted author, said, "It takes as much courage to have tried and failed as it does to have tried and succeeded." Stop letting your fear of failure keep you from enjoying the process of living and learning.

How can I get the most out of high school (without going crazy)?

"Just be open to new experiences," says Keelyn Welch, a senior at Swampscott High School in Swampscott, Massachusetts. Many of the junior high students we've talked with are psyched about the many opportunities they'll have in high school. Jeff Toohig says, "I'm looking forward to expanding my horizons and meeting new friends." Joey Schmidt is equally enthusiastic: "I'm looking forward to meeting new people, to having good teachers, and to playing sports at the high school level."

Rebecca Stevens, a seventh grader at the Calhoun School in New York City, says, "I'm looking forward to new privileges. And I'm looking forward to being on varsity sports teams and to having a choice of community service projects. I like the idea that I'll be meeting older people and that I'll get new teachers."

To squeeze every drop of juice out of high school may not be possible, but you can become very involved — without overextending yourself. First and most important, don't misuse your time. Hanging out in front of the tube every afternoon for hour upon hour is not the way to make the most of your teenage years. High school is the time in your life to take advantage of sports and clubs. You're being handed these opportunities on a silver platter. Don't waste them.

Second, assume responsibility. Be a leader. Don't think that to be "cool," you have to pretend to be apathetic. If you feel strongly about something, speak out. High school is one of the few times in your life when you can do so freely and openly, without having any responsibility toward anyone or anything but yourself. Moreover, insecurity levels in teenagers run pretty high, and your peers are looking for someone to look up to — why can't you be that person?

Third, set goals for yourself, whether they be on a daily, weekly, or monthly basis. Meeting those goals, even if they're relatively trivial, will make your time spent juggling worthwhile. Fourth, don't lose sight of reality. No matter how many times your parents, friends, and teachers tell you that high school is to be taken seriously, everyone knows, deep down, that high school is a time to be cherished . . . thoroughly.

What can I do to "get away from it all"?

Students tell us that their best method of escaping and defusing stress is to have a friend to turn to who is an objective and unbiased "translator" of what's happening at the time. Some teens find solace in befriending a senior citizen in the neighborhood or in a local nursing home. They've been amazed at the wisdom these friends can offer.

Other teens recommend finding a hobby. Channeling your energies into something that gives you pleasure and takes your mind off of other things is a great way to get a more balanced outlook on life. It doesn't matter whether you garden, collect signatures, tinker with cars, or write short stories. The key is to find something that excites you and gives you something to look forward to every day.

Sometimes it feels as though life is just too unpredictable and there's nobody and nothing I can count on consistently. Whom do other teens turn to?

A lot of the kids we've spoken to belong to youth groups at their churches and synagogues. You can do that, too, even if you're not all that religious. Contrary to what you might think, church groups don't necessarily sit around talking about religion. Rather, they organize various activities and outings and discuss a broad range of topics that are of concern to teens these days. Students who are involved in youth groups tell us that sometimes these groups seem like the only "constants" in their lives. No matter what's happening at school or with friends or family, the church or synagogue is always there for them.

There's a lot to be said for bouncing ideas off of people who are going through the same things as you. It might make you feel better to realize that you're not going through everything alone. And you might find someone who has lived through what you're experiencing and can offer some pretty good advice. If there's no youth group in your religious community, talk to your religious leader (minister, priest, or rabbi). He or she is trained in giving advice that can be soothing to both the mind and the spirit. Talk to him or her regularly — set up a time when you know you can reach out, either by telephone or in person.

There are also other youth clubs in the community to consider. The YMCA/YWCA, the YMHA/YWHA, and the Boys' and Girls' Clubs are just three of the organizations that provide youths with activities and a sense of belonging. Look in the Yellow Pages or ask your guidance counselor about what's available in your area.

hs adviser

Making the Most of High School

Kristin Kaldor, a 1990 graduate of Georgetown University, reflects on her high school experience at Junction City Senior High School in Junction City, Kansas:

When I started high school, I remember telling myself that I was going to try to break out of the group of friends that I had in junior high and become more involved. I wanted to meet different people and get a different perspective on things. So, in high school I ran for student government and joined a ton of clubs. And I found that not only did the clubs introduce me to different people, but also that one of the clubs, which ran the foreign exchange student program, really broadened my horizons in terms of what I wanted to do after high school.

I think I always knew, deep down, that I wanted to leave Kansas when it came time to go to college. But all of my friends were, for the most part, content to go to Kansas State or the University of Kansas and to pretty much stay in Kansas for the rest of their lives. The experiences that I had in high school really convinced me that I wanted to be different. They challenged me to break out of that stay-in-Kansas mentality. Through the foreign exchange club, I became close friends with many foreign students who brought a new and more cultural aspect into Junction City.

The competition wasn't really fierce at my high school, although I really stressed out a lot because I put a ton of pressure on myself to do well. Socially, there were a lot of cliques, which tended to breed some hostility and frustration. We were a very athletic school, and the most competition among students had to do with athletics rather than schoolwork. In retrospect, even though Junction City is so small, high school was a great experience and a *lot* of fun. It's really what you make of it, no matter what the circumstances are.

Twenty-Five Top-Rated Hiding Places*

☆ Your bed
☆ A bathtub or hot tub
☆ A library — preferably with a trashy novel
☆ Your local junk-food haven
☆ Under your favorite tree or in an old tree house (suburban kids)
☆ Your favorite stoop (city kids)
☆ The movies
☆ The mall
☆ The roof of a building or house with a great view
☆ The ballpark
☆ A museum or art gallery
☆ The gym
☆ A playground with swings
☆ A pier or dock
☆ A best friend's house
☆ Your grandparents' house
☆ A farm or riding stable
☆ A favorite place you used to go to as a child
☆ A local college's student union or reading room
☆ An outdoor café
☆ A bus or train
☆ An empty classroom
☆ A zoo or aquarium
☆ The lobby of a hotel
☆ A park

* This list was created by the delegates to the National High School Reporter weekend. P

Family Ties

**"A lot of kids think grown-ups don't care or
don't listen — but I just don't think that's true."**

Chad Fisher, an eleventh grader at Abraham Lincoln
High School in Des Moines, Iowa

Q & A: PARENTAL PET PEEVES

Why do my parents continue to treat me like a small child?

If you think adolescence is tough, imagine how hard it is for your parents
to see you maturing, gaining independence, and developing into an adult.
What it boils down to is that you simply don't need them as much as you
used to, and that can be difficult for a parent to come to grips with. Be
prepared to give them plenty of time to get used to the fact that you're
becoming an independent person. And be prepared to prove to them that
you're mature enough to be treated like a responsible teenager.

    If you feel that your parents are treating you like a child because they
don't trust your judgment, ask yourself whether you'd be willing to take
total responsibility for every move you make. Would you act any differently if your parents weren't going to be there to bail you out whenever

you screwed up? There may be times when you lapse into a childlike frame of mind, and that's probably what your parents are judging you by. There are specific things you can do, however, to prove to your parents that you are, in fact, growing up:

•Give up your Friday or Saturday night activities with your friends once in a while and suggest an activity with your parents. You'll probably end up enjoying yourself, and your parents will see your initiative as indicative of a "good sense of judgment."

•When you go to a party on a Friday night, don't sleep until 2:00 P.M. the next day. Get up at a reasonable hour and fill your parents in on what went on the night before. If there were drugs or alcohol at the party, tell them — and make it clear that you handled the situation responsibly.

•If you find yourself unable to get home after a party because your "ride" is too drunk to drive, call home and ask your parents to come and get you. They may be angry that you and your friends were drinking, but at least they'll know that you weren't stupid enough to get into a car with a drunk driver.

•Always call and let your parents know where you are, especially if you're going to be out past your curfew.

My parents and I just can't seem to connect. Is that unusual?

Everyone knows that communication — whether it be in the business world, between nations, or within a family — is the first step toward dealing with problems. Unfortunately, communication between parents and kids these days is getting tougher and tougher, what with divorced parents living apart, kids shuffling between different homes on certain days of the week, and the ever-increasing pace of life. "A lot of teenagers are growing up in either 'blended' families or single-parent families these days," says Cheryl Smith, mother of Rachel (thirteen) and Roland (sixteen), who lives in Newburyport, Massachusetts. "It's important for parents to communicate effectively with their kids and vice versa, and almost as important for parents to communicate with other parents."

One reason you may be failing to connect with your folks is the lack of time you spend together. If the only time you're with your parents is when you watch TV, you need to make a change. Blow off your friends for a weekend or two and hang around with Mom and Dad instead. Ask them questions about your relatives or about when they were kids. Find out how they got along with their parents — it may give you a clue as to why they're the way they are. A couple of days of buddying up to your parents isn't going to change your life, but it may be the start of a change for the better in how you communicate.

My parents just told me they're getting a divorce. Is there anything I can do to stop it?

Teenagers whose parents have split up tell us that their first instinct upon hearing of their mom and dad's imminent divorce was to try their best to get them back together again. Some actually succeeded, only to prolong further everyone's misery and merely postpone the inevitable breakup.

We spoke to a student at UCLA who can certainly empathize with what you're going through. She says, "I first sensed that there were problems when I was about thirteen years old, because my parents' bedroom door was closed all the time. They had *never* closed the door to their room, and our family had always been really open with one another. The minute I sensed that something was wrong, I approached my mom and asked her if everything was okay. Now I wish that I hadn't. I should have waited it out, because I think that my asking about it made the situation worse. I felt such a huge sense of loss, and all I cared about in the world was making sure that my parents got back together. I stopped caring about school, my clothes, myself in general. I couldn't handle the fact that our routine was broken. My dad wasn't coming home the way he used to and sitting down at the dinner table with us. We weren't spending Saturdays together anymore. The breaking of routine left me with a huge void in my life, and I couldn't cope with it at all."

When you feel that someone is causing you so much hurt, it's difficult not to lash out at him or her and become bitter and angry. Most teenagers we've spoken with say they took revenge on their parents during and after their divorce by trying to make them as miserable as they themselves were —and they ended up regretting it.

"In my case, anger, bitterness, and a feeling of abandonment, because they were left unaddressed, came out in self-destruction later in life," says a 1989 graduate of Duke University whose parents were divorced when she was eleven. "The major source of trouble in dealing with my parents' divorce was that no one ever took the time to explain the problems to me. As a result of this, I convinced myself that the divorce was my fault, despite the fact that my parents never implied anything of the sort. I have been left with a feeling of things being unresolvable in my life, as if my actions don't really matter."

Coping with your parents' divorce is going to be a really difficult thing for you to do, but by the time they tell you about it, it's probably too late to change their minds. If you try to keep them together, you might end up making things much worse. What you need to understand is that your parents' decision to divorce doesn't mean they don't love you as much as they always have. It just means that they can't live with each other any longer. It's probably difficult for you to understand how someone who claims to love you so much is willing to cause you such great pain. The thing to remember is that your parents are hurting as much as — or more than — you are.

The best thing for you to do right now is talk about what's bothering you. A sense of shame and embarrassment is often associated with divorce, and those feelings are made worse by parents who encourage their children to remain "hush-hush" about family problems. "Parents' telling their kids not to talk about the divorce is the worst thing they could do," says the student from Duke. "Let out what you're feeling. Talk about it without feeling shame and, most important, know that you are not responsible for your parents' problems. If you don't feel comfortable talking to a friend, talk to your school psychologist or social worker."

Is there such a thing as a "normal" family?

Many teenagers compare their families with those around them, which may appear from the outside to be the "perfect American families." In truth, this perception may be the "perfect American myth." These days, practically anything goes on the family circuit. Just about every family has its share of problems behind that white picket fence. How could they not? Bring together any group of people, whether it be at school, work, camp, wherever, and there are bound to be personality clashes and strife. Why should it be any different when it comes to families?

The truth is, family relations are even more problem-prone than friendships. You can choose your friends, but there's nothing you can do about your family. You're stuck with them, like it or not. "The weirdest day of my year is always Thanksgiving, when my whole family gets together," says Norma,* an eleventh grader from Seattle, Washington. "Bring together *that* motley crew and you could do a case study. No wonder everyone dreads it, but there's nothing anyone can do. We just suffer through it, and it would be pretty comical if it weren't so sad that none of us get along." But in defense of families, and parents in particular, is Melissa Marshall, a freshman at the National Cathedral School in Washington, D.C. Melissa thinks that parents, and families in general, get picked on too much by some kids, and really deserve a break!

The idealized version of a family consisting of a working dad; cookie-baking mom; 2.4 happy, healthy kids; and a dog named Ruff hasn't survived the changes in our society. Don't worry if your family isn't like that. If it were, you'd be completely abnormal.

How can I get my parents to really listen to me?

Wouldn't it be nice if your parents could spend a week inside your mind and body and have to deal with what you go through on a daily basis? Maybe they'd understand you better if they went to school and dealt with all of the highs and lows of being a teenager in the 1990s.

On the flip side, your parents probably wish that you could spend a day in their lives so you'd pull yourself out of your teenage frame of mind and see that they're dealing with a lot of pressures and issues themselves. If it seems as though your parents aren't listening to you, ask yourself if you're really listening to them. Chances are, you probably aren't, and giving it a try might work wonders. No one's saying you have to agree with everything your folks say, but if you cut them some slack, it'll be a lot easier to get the lines of communication open. This doesn't mean that your parents will automatically agree to your plans to spend the summer skateboarding across the country. But knowing a bit more about what's going on in your life might make them more sympathetic to your side of the story. You'll at least have broken through the first barrier.

If you think you've given your parents a fair shot at listening to them and you don't feel that they're returning the favor, sit them down and start from scratch. Don't make it a big-deal confrontation. Tell them you're worried that you and they are "growing apart" — they'll have watched enough "Cosby" to know that it's time to hear what you have to say. Then talk to them about what school is like, about teachers, students, competition, jealousies, prejudices, whatever. The more honest you are with them, the more willing they'll be to listen.

Why does it seem as though my parents don't care about me?

This is a very difficult and individual question, but what it boils down to is that parents seem to strike out with teenagers whichever way they swing the bat. Many of you complain that your parents are overprotective and that you wish they'd give you more independence. But just as many of you are upset by the fact that your parents are never around and just don't seem to care about you one way or the other. With the large number of single parents and dual-income households out there these days, many teens have parents who leave the house early in the morning and return fairly late at night, too tired to talk to or even listen to their kids.

One of our friends àt The Ethel Walker School in Simsbury, Connecticut, says, "I have to try hard to get the attention of my parents. I really need to talk to them, and sometimes they don't seem to hear me. They're busy working, and it depends a lot on the tone I use. But even when I don't get them to listen to me, I still need them."

If your parents are not there for you as much as you wish they were, it's very important for you to realize that they aren't leaving you alone because they don't care about you. Kids who claim that their parents are overbearing and overprotective (and there are many of you out there) will tell you that you should be flattered that your parents trust you enough to give you so much freedom. "Hands off" parenting can cause a teenager to feel unloved, but in the long run you'll be better equipped and more self-sufficient than someone whose parents did everything for him or her.

If the lack of attention from your parents is really bothering you, though, it would make sense to talk to a counselor or social worker at school. Don't be embarrassed about it — that's what they're there for. They may be able to help you make your parents understand that you're not getting enough of what you need. Adults aren't always too "with it" when it comes to their kids. You might have to help them along.

How can I persuade my parents to let me have a pet? They say that animals are too much of a responsibility.

Your mom and dad may have a valid reason for being against your having a pet. Do you live in an apartment with no back yard? Are your parents unable to afford the expenses a pet will incur? If either of these is the case, you — and the pet — would be better off waiting until your circumstances change. If there are no other obstacles to pet ownership, however, your parents may simply not believe you're ready or willing to take on the responsibility of caring for a dog or cat. And believe us, it involves a lot more than feeding the animal and letting it out the back door once in a while. A pet requires a great deal of attention and affection, and it absolutely changes the owner's lifestyle. Many new pet owners claim that having a pet teaches them a lot about what it would be like to have a child. You're responsible for the pet's well-being twenty-four hours a day, 365 days a year.

Many parents fear that their kids will lose interest in the family pet and that the parents will end up having to care for it for many years to come. So, if you're positive you're ready to take on this responsibility, your best bet is to prove to your parents that (1) you understand just what you're getting yourself into, and (2) you are willing and able to take full responsibility for the pet's care. But, be warned, if your behavior up to this point has been immature and irresponsible, your parents aren't likely to believe your promises, no matter how good an act you put on. In that case — or if your parents refuse your request to get a pet for any other reason — consider playing with your friend's pet as much as you can. Or start your own dog-walking business, which will earn you some money while you're at it. There are a lot of busy people out there who would be more than willing to have a responsible teenager take some pet-related chores off their hands.

My friends think I'm crazy because I worry more about my dog, Benjamin, than I do about my brother or my parents. Is this normal?

Absolutely. There are a lot of people out there who form incredibly strong bonds with their pets. And why not? Benjamin probably is physically closer to you than anyone else in the world — you may hug your parents or brother, but we'll bet Benjamin is the only one who snuggles on your lap for hours on end. And who else do you know whose primary goal in life is to please you? No doubt your parents and brother love you very much, but there will always be conflicts between you. Caring parents set down rules for their kids, and even though you know they're for your own good, you may not always like them. Benjamin, on the other hand, follows your rules and loves you unconditionally. Do you know anyone else who wags his tail and jumps in excitement every time you come through the door?

So tell your friends to chill out. Loving your pet is a normal and positive reaction that doesn't take away from your relationships with the human members of your family. Anyone who doesn't understand that must never have owned a pet.

hs adviser

Parents Speak Out

Erin Granger Siegal, mother of Elizabeth, seventeen, Fort Lee, New Jersey:

What is Elizabeth's biggest complaint about you, and what is your response to that complaint?
Elizabeth was convinced that I didn't trust her, because I set a pretty strict curfew. In response to that, I finally looked back to when I was seventeen, and when I did so, I found that I was being much more strict with my daughter than my parents had been with me. I realized that she deserved more trust from me . . . and things have been much better since.

What would you like your daughter to know?
I certainly trust my daughter and I want her to know that when I pry, it's because I really want to know about everything that's going on in her life. I feel much better knowing the truth, even if it's difficult for me to handle.

What worries you about kids today?
I worry about how insecure a lot of kids are. So many teenagers who have great personalities and are smart and attractive compare themselves with others, put themselves down constantly, and think that they're not good enough in anything they do. I wish they would realize how much they have to offer.

Bruce Cohn, father of Meredyth, fifteen, and Jason, eighteen, North Miami Beach, Florida:

What's the best thing about being a parent?
Being a parent is never easy. Kids don't have any idea how difficult it can be to be a parent. Many kids these days think they're more liberated than we are, and they're too sophisticated for their own good.

Why? Because in this day and age of computers and high technology, they feel that they're completely in control and able to do almost anything. They want to take steps three and four before they finish steps one and two.

Do you accept your kids the way they are?
I have a hard time agreeing on certain things with my kids, and I don't think that my opinions about certain issues will ever change. I am trying to respect what they choose to do, and I think that that is the most important thing. But I don't necessarily have to agree with them.

David Miller, father of Emily, seventeen, Incline Village, Nevada:

What is your daughter's biggest complaint about you, and what is your response to that complaint?
Her complaint is most definitely that I am too restrictive. She has had set curfews, and I make it clear that I want to meet the boys that she dates. If I don't care for one of her boyfriends, I tell her so. Emily would like all the freedom in the world, but my wife and I feel that she needs a certain amount of structure and guidance in her life. We often have to answer the question "Why?" with respect to restrictions, and our answer is simply that it's for her own good, to keep her out of trouble. And it's because we love her.

What do you think is the most important thing about being a parent?
Being involved in their lives and maintaining a loving and kind attitude is essential to a teenager's well-being. Sharing your time, whether it involves bonding through sports or getting involved in their school activities, is one of the most important aspects of parenthood.

Ten Things Your Parents Ought to Tell You . . . But Might Not

☆ Stand up for what you believe in . . . no matter what.

☆ Enjoy life — this isn't a dress rehearsal.

☆ We wouldn't change a thing about you.

☆ *Every* move you make now will play a part in your future.

☆ You're going to think that your first serious boyfriend/girlfriend will be the person you'll marry.

☆ The more popular, successful, and rich you are, the more people there are who are going to dislike you.

☆ With friends come enemies.

☆ Don't mix beer and wine.

☆ Authority figures aren't always right.

☆ We're just as scared as you are. **P**

Siblings

"Siblings are great to learn responsibilities and share things. Having siblings helps to build togetherness."

Margie Abdelrazek, an eleventh grader at Bearden
High School in Knoxville, Tennessee

Q & A: BIG BROTHER/BIG SISTER IS WATCHING

My siblings and I compete in everything — from how much attention we get from our parents to grades to sports. Are we ever going to overcome this competitiveness and become friends?

Siblings, whether younger or older, get mixed reviews from the high school students we've spoken with around the country. Most of you have told us that your siblings fall into one of two extremes: practically your best friend or huge pains in the neck. Very few of you have brothers and sisters whom you consider to be just sort of "there."

No matter how well you get along, though, unless you and your siblings are complete opposites and are interested in totally different things, there's bound to be some competition. How should you deal with it? "Don't fight it. It can be healthy, and it can challenge you both to do your best at everything," says Leo Shin, a sophomore at Teaneck High School in Teaneck, New Jersey. Experts agree that sibling rivalry is normal, provided it doesn't get out of hand.

Children with divorced parents and teens who have parents who aren't home that much report that they and their siblings compete for their parents' attention. "My younger sister and I really vie for our father's attention since our parents are divorced and he's not around all the time," says Ashley Bryan. "We're much less competitive about our mother, since she's with us so much more frequently." This is an issue that has to be worked out between kids and parents, but parents should take the initiative in letting their kids know that they are equally loved and that there is no need for them to compete against one another. If you think your brother or sister is hogging all your dad's or mom's time, speak up — to your parent. Yelling at your siblings won't get you anywhere; explaining your feelings to your parent might.

The best way to combat the feeling that you're always being compared with your siblings, especially in athletics or academics, is to carve a different niche for yourself. Just because your older sister is a star tennis player doesn't mean you have to follow in her footsteps. And just because your older brother is the state math champion doesn't mean you have to join your school's algorithm club. Try something new, something that you like, and you'll have taken your first step toward diminishing sibling rivalry in your home.

How can I be a good role model for my younger siblings?

Even if you know you've made certain mistakes and you don't want your younger siblings to do the same, realize that making mistakes is a part of growing up. To a certain extent, your siblings are just going to have to learn through experience. Ashley Bryan says, "My younger sister and I talk about clothes, boys, where to go to high school, what teachers to take, makeup, hair, and friends. But as far as philosophical things go, things that I've learned along the way, I think she'll learn them on her own. She needs to, just like every teenager needs to." Jessica Berkeley adds, "My sister and I aren't that much alike. Therefore, my advice and experiences are not necessarily applicable to her situation. I try to help her but certainly don't consider myself her best adviser." And, as important, while a nurturing instinct may be natural for you, don't assume that your siblings are going to want your advice all the time.

Some younger siblings we've spoken with claim that their older brothers and sisters tend to offer unwanted advice a bit too frequently. "It can be annoying to have someone telling you what to do and what not to do all the time . . . that's what parents are for," says Linda,* a senior from Junction City, Kansas. Older siblings have to be particularly careful to remember that they are siblings, not parents or guardians. "My sister moved back into the house after college," says Leo Shin, "and instead of sticking up for me, she started siding with my parents and bossing me around all the time. That was really hard to deal with, especially after she'd been gone for so long." Dana Wolf, a sophomore at the Hebrew Academy of the Five Towns and Rockaway in Cedarhurst, Long Island, is older sister to three — all girls, and all highly verbal. "Sometimes I have to remind myself that we have a mother and a father and that I am not my sisters' mother. It's hard, though, because I am protective and want to help them avoid difficulties I've encountered. Also, it's tough for me not to become the mean older sister since I end up criticizing them a lot . . . especially when they don't want to listen the first time I suggest something."

If you want to help your younger siblings to make the right decisions, the best thing you can do is lead by example. Chances are that just by being around you and observing your actions, your siblings will pick up some good habits and aspirations. If you notice that your younger siblings aren't at all like you, chalk it up to inherent personality differences and do your best to accept them as individuals with different interests from yours. You'll gain their respect by showing them respect.

I genuinely hate my brother. And he hates me. Everyone says that we'll outgrow this, but I don't particularly care what happens once we don't have to live under the same roof. Is it that uncommon to have a sibling who makes you crazy and sick?

It's not at all uncommon for siblings to go through periods in which they claim to hate each other. In fact, it's pretty normal. But it would be surprising if you and your brother hated each other for the rest of your lives. At certain ages, siblings will go to any lengths to make each other's lives miserable, from eavesdropping to mimicking to putting rodents in each other's beds. Think of Kevin Arnold's older brother on "The Wonder Years." What a pain in the neck! But eventually, even Kevin and Wayne will learn to appreciate each other.

What usually determines the nature of sibling relationships is age. Kids in their early teens are generally pretty defensive, and this shows in their relationships with siblings, as well as with parents and teachers. And few kids at that age have the depth of understanding and maturity necessary to work problems out. So things just keep getting worse and worse, and siblings do anything and everything they can think of to drive each other nuts.

However, living with someone you hate can make life pretty miserable. If you and your brother can learn even to tolerate each other, you'll both be much happier. Maybe it's time to get out the white flag and declare a few neutral zones. An easy way to break down his defenses is to ask him for advice. At least you'll have made an effort. And the more time you spend talking, the less time he'll have to booby-trap your room.

One more thing, which your parents, especially, may be reluctant to tell you: You can't choose your relatives in the way you choose your friends. And you may well end up with a brother, a sister, or a cousin whom you'd prefer never to have heard of, let alone be related to. That said, understand that your parents will rarely see things exactly as you do. Parents typically love their children and are somewhat blinded by this affection from observing the stuff you see.

How can I make the most of my older siblings' experience?

Older brothers and sisters can be an excellent source of information that you might not feel comfortable getting from your parents or friends. Adam Kanner tells us, "My older sister really showed me the ropes about everything. I look back on a lot of stuff and wonder what I would have done if she hadn't prepared me for it." He adds, "My sister can't quite believe the stuff I'm allowed to do as a sophomore, since our parents were so much more overprotective of her. That parents are not as cautious in the way they handle younger children is probably one of the best things about having an older brother or sister."

Getting advice from older siblings can be like taking a trip into the future and learning how to avoid mistakes before you actually make them. Ask your brothers and sisters a lot of questions. Even if they haven't experienced certain things, they may know someone who has.

If you have an older sibling who's in college or who doesn't live with you, try to visit him or her as much as possible so you can get a firsthand feel for what college life or life in the real world is like. Establish a trust so that, even if you are a lot younger, your sibling will talk to you as a peer. No matter what your older brother or sister has done — traveled, gone to college, joined the military — you can learn a lot from hearing about those experiences.

My father recently married a much younger woman, and now they're going to have a baby. On one hand, I'm happy for them, but on the other hand, I'm angry. I live with my mom and I know she's upset about the whole thing. How should I be feeling about my new half brother or half sister?

Your anger is normal — face it, you're jealous and you probably resent your father and his new wife for what they've been putting your mother through. But you must realize that even though your father is having another child, it will not in any way affect the way he feels about you. In fact, he's probably relying on you to help out with the new baby and lend a lot of support. The baby is lucky to have a much older sibling — take the child under your wing from the very beginning and watch him or her grow and mature. If you take a part in his or her developmental process, it will be very rewarding for you in the long run.

One thing you especially need to prepare yourself for is the way your father will react to the new baby. Very often, a man who has more children later in life will find that he devotes more time to them than he did to his older children. This doesn't mean he loves the new baby any more. It simply reflects the fact that he's probably settled in a career and has more discretion over the way he spends his time. Also, he may regret having been unable to spend a lot of time with his older kids as they grew up. This time, he doesn't want to make the same mistakes.

Don't resent the fact that your dad has improved his parenting skills. After all, it's your brother or sister who is reaping the rewards. And, by the way, that's how you should think of the new child — as a brother or sister. Thinking of this new member of your family as a half sibling will put a barrier between you two that is utterly unnecessary. How you treat the baby will set the tone for your lifelong relationship. Make it a loving one.

Why do stepsiblings seem to have such trouble getting along with one another?

A divorce or death of a parent is always traumatic for the children involved, and sometimes this trauma is compounded by a parent's remarriage to someone who already has kids. Even the Brady Bunch took a while to get used to one another. If your stepsiblings don't live with you, they may not play a very big part in your life at all. It may just bug you that your mom or dad is living with and taking care of kids other than you.

It's an entirely different story if you're actually living with stepsiblings. All the problems common to relationships between brothers and sisters are compounded by the resentment that comes with major change. If there is undeniable animosity between you and your stepsiblings, talking to your parents about it will help. Parents, especially those who have recently gone through a divorce and remarriage, can be so caught up in their own lives that they simply don't realize what their kids are going through. More often than not, you'll find that jealousy is the root of the problem. You might feel as though your father should be giving more attention to you than to your stepbrother because you're your father's "real" son. Or your stepsister may resent you because you're prettier than she is and more popular in school. But all of these differences can be overcome. Be aware that your stepsiblings are going through the same trauma as you and try to understand that it might take longer for some kids to adjust to new situations than others. As you grow and mature you'll probably learn to appreciate these new members of your family. Until then, don't take out your resentment on them. Work it out with your parents instead.

Actually, not all stepfamilies are riddled with conflict. Ashley Bryan, who has a stepbrother and two half brothers, in addition to her sister, says, "All of us genuinely love one another. It may sound corny, but, whenever we're together, the five of us enjoy one another, even our little brothers who are still in elementary school. Sure, my stepbrother, George, who is a senior in college, sometimes gives me crazy advice, but I appreciate how much he cares about my sister and me." She adds, "I still remember when Dad took me to meet him for the first time — I was about eight. He was so cute and friendly then, and now. And I miss my little brothers when I'm in Texas and they're in New York."

hs adviser

Advice from Siblings

"Be careful with whom you become involved . . . don't have relationships with just anyone." —Emily Loyd, Harpeth Hall, Nashville, Tennessee

"Be patient with Mom and Dad. If you have a problem with them, work it out by talking with them. Don't keep it inside." —Tom Wallace, Bullis School, Potomac, Maryland

"Make sure you keep your good friends. Your best friends are ones that you can depend on and trust." —Alexandra Meckel, The Spence School, New York, New York

"Do everything you can to live life to the fullest. Don't be intimidated by anything. And get involved." —Maria Rosel, Paramus Catholic Girls High School, Paramus, New Jersey

"Always listen to what Mom and Dad say. If you don't, you'll really end up paying your dues and regretting it." —Rebecca Bagatelle, East Brunswick High School, East Brunswick, New Jersey

"Keep realistic views about the world." —Melissa Maeurer, Garden City Middle School, Garden City, New York

"My little sister should know that I'll always be there for her. Also, she should be careful with dating, and she shouldn't listen to everything the guys say, especially with AIDS going around." —Sandy Levin, La Guardia High School, New York, New York

"Keep trying as hard as you can and always have a positive outlook on life. Being negative will get you nowhere." —Jennifer Singer, Upper Dublin High School, Fort Washington, Pennsylvania

Big Bro, Little Sis

Caroline Portny, a ninth grader at The Spence School in New York City, and David Portny, a freshman at Colgate University, talk about their brother/sister relationship.

David: Caroline and I have had a great relationship ever since we were really young. As her older brother, I was around at all of her birthday parties, I helped her with her schoolwork when she needed it, and we always played games and watched TV together after school. Our relationship was like that until she hit the sixth or seventh grade. Then she started socializing with members of the opposite sex. The only thing that bothered me was the fact that her boyfriends would call up and say all kinds of obnoxious things. (That was before I scared them off with threats of violence.) When Caroline was twelve, things became a little bit touchy and she was sort of difficult to get along with — but I guess she was probably going through a rough time.

I've always thought that it is very important to support Caroline in everything she does. When we have confrontations with our parents, I come to her defense and she comes to mine. I think she has always looked up to me, and I've always wanted to be there to answer questions about whatever it is that I can give her advice on. I don't encourage her to do everything I did or experienced. There are certain things that I do recommend that Caroline do. However, those choices are up to her. If I can help her in making those choices, I will. I'll do anything in my power to assist my sister in whatever she chooses to do.

Caroline: I've never expected David to bail me out of things, but he has really paved the way for me, especially when it comes to my parents. He always sticks up for me. Well, maybe not always. I guess only when he knows it's in my best interest. One of the best things about David is that he doesn't take a position on how I should handle a given situation; he encourages me to make the decision on my own. Plus, I get advice from him about the way I look when I'm going out, what I'm wearing, etc. It's nice to have it from a guy's perspective. But it works both ways — I give him the same type of advice. As we've grown older, our age difference (four years) seems to have grown smaller and smaller. Now that I'm in high school it seems as though David and I are on more equal turf as far as our crowds of friends and stuff go.

We've always been so close, and when he was going away to college this year I thought I'd be crying all the time. I miss him a lot, but it hasn't been as bad as I thought it would be. We still talk a lot and have stayed close. **P**

Your Best Friend

"My high school friends are cool because they like to do the same things I like to do. I'm definitely going to stay in touch with them for a long time."

Charles Crismon, a twelfth grader at Kahuku
High School in Kahuku, Hawaii

Q & A: THE UPS AND DOWNS OF FRIENDSHIP

Is it normal to be jealous of my best friend?

It happens to the best of us: Your best friend is smart and beautiful and has gorgeous clothes, a convertible sports car, and guys swooning over her. Or, he can pick up a basketball for the first time ever and shoot ten swish shots in a row, has every piece of high-tech equipment known to man, and has women oohing and aahing over his every burp in the cafeteria. Who wouldn't have a huge inferiority complex after witnessing this inequality day in and day out?

It's perfectly normal to wonder why you didn't get the luck of the draw and have all the advantages of your friend. But keep in mind that jealousy can be a good thing, in moderate amounts. It can challenge you to be your best and to develop things you do better than your "perfect" friend. Make the most of the fact that your friend has nice things — you can reap the benefits of them also.

If you find your jealousy getting out of control, though, try to put everything into perspective. You'll have a hard time being happy if you go through life comparing yourself with other people all the time. And how do you know your friend isn't jealous of you? After all, you must be doing something right or you wouldn't be this person's best friend. Right?

What characteristics do people look for in a best friend?

"My best friend can listen without overadvising. She's really supportive," says Ashley Bryan. "I like to be able to talk about anything without feeling guilty. I had one friend who didn't have parents, and whenever I said something bad about my parents, she'd say, 'At least you have parents.' I couldn't handle that." Amanda Abraham, an eighth grader at Garden City Middle School in Garden City, New York, tells us that her friends must be on her wavelength. "They have to have the same interests as me and be able to talk about anything at any given time."

Most of you have told us that what's really important in a friendship is mutual interests. Ron Palmon says, "At the beginning of high school, I was friends with most of the guys on the sports teams because I played sports. Then as high school progressed, the courses and extracurriculars became more specialized, and I found that my friends were those who were in the same classes and activities as me." Adam Goodman, a sophomore at James Madison High School in Vienna, Virginia, tells us that his friends are down-to-earth and not cocky. He looks for people he can joke around with, who aren't too serious.

What if my parents don't like my friend(s)?

Parents have a tendency to be unenthusiastic about kids they don't know really well, especially if the teenager doesn't dress or act the way they want you to. Parents also tend to have a "network" that breeds gossip about the "bad" kids in town, so they may have preconceived notions about kids whom they've never even met. Do your best to have your friend around your parents as much as possible so your parents can see your friend's positive qualities.

Remember, though, that sometimes parents do know best. Dan Diman, a junior at Oregon Episcopal School in Portland, Oregon, says, "My parents didn't really care for one of my friends, and, before it even became an issue between us, I realized that I pretty much agreed with my parents' opinions about him." As much as you hate to admit it, your parents' sixth sense might really be on target some of the time.

When asked if you have ever had a problem with your parents about one of your friends, the large majority of you said no. It seems that parents these days trust their kids' judgment when it comes to choosing whom to hang out with. And they realize that if your friend really is a problem waiting to happen, you'll come to your senses sooner or later.

How can I make my parents and others believe that my friends of the opposite sex are just friends, nothing more?

Parents seem to think that the minute girls and guys hang out together, they're up to something. But it couldn't be further from the truth. Remember where your parents are coming from, though. When they went to school, there may even have been separate entrances for girls and boys. No wonder they think it's odd that you can interact in a non-date setting.

It might be hard for your parents to understand how much the two sexes have in common these days. There simply aren't so many things anymore that are exclusively male or female. Girls can be interested in cars and science; guys can get into poetry and folk music. A few of you have told us that your best friends are, in fact, members of the opposite sex. And that's great. Don't let anyone make you feel as though you're doing something wrong. Having a friend of the opposite sex is a great learning experience. You're going to have to learn to understand each other someday, so why not start young?

If your parents persist in giving you grief about your friendship, make sure your friend is around the house as much as possible when your parents are there. That way, they'll see that you really are just friends. Don't expect them to forget your differences entirely, however. If you two vanish into your room all afternoon, it's sure to raise eyebrows and, unless your parents are completely convinced there will never be anything between you, you can kiss those plans for a camping trip goodbye.

hs adviser

College Students Reflect on Maintaining High School Friendships

"To keep in touch with your high school friends, you have to make sure that you see them when you come home for weekends. Otherwise, you know you'll completely lose touch. I don't think there's any way to prevent drifting apart to some extent, though, because college is a new and different life, and you spend most of your time concerned with that." —Michael Sluchan, University of Pennsylvania (Collegiate School, New York, New York)

"I had a very close group of three friends in high school — two girlfriends and my boyfriend — and we remained pretty reserved and separate from the rest of the grade, which basically made up one huge clique. When we went off to college, my boyfriend and I went our separate ways. I got together with one of my girlfriends on the first vacation of freshman year in college, and we totally couldn't relate to one another because our lives were so different from what they had been. She was talking all about herself and her new life in college, and I was talking about myself, and neither of us was willing to listen to what the other was saying. My third friend, who was really my best friend in high school, has remained one of my very good friends. Even though we're at different colleges, we're still interested in each other's lives. That's the key to retaining your high school friendships." —Melissa Cotler, Skidmore College (Trumbull High School, Trumbull, Connecticut)

"It's really difficult to keep in touch with your friends after high school. All of my friends go to different schools around the country, so I really have to make an effort to keep in touch with them. For example, when my school has something special going on, I invite them up for the weekend. But there's still a gap between us, as though we're all going in different directions." —Larry Pacheco Jr., University of Colorado (Iver C. Ranum High School, Denver, Colorado)

How to Drive Your Best Friend Crazy

Girls

☆ Go out and buy the exact outfit she had on yesterday.

☆ Be there to listen when she's down in the dumps. When things are going well for her, flee from the face of the earth with your hands over your ears.

☆ Tell her you didn't study a bit for that huge calculus exam — then get an A on it.

☆ When she complains about her parents, take their side.

☆ Borrow her favorite sweater for the date you're having with the guy she likes.

☆ Get lipstick all over her favorite sweater.

☆ Tell the guy she likes that she likes him.

Guys

☆ Challenge him to a one-on-one game and beat him at it . . . in front of his girl-friend.

☆ Tell his parents that you'd never dream of letting your folks give you an allowance — that a part-time job teaches responsibility.

☆ Flirt with his sister.

☆ Borrow his all-pro football and let your dog chew it up.

☆ Tell his coach that he didn't really have the flu yesterday afternoon but couldn't miss an important soap opera episode.

☆ Borrow his car and leave your fast-food leftovers all over the back seat.

☆ Borrow his car and use all the gas without replacing it. P

Do You Want to Dance?

by Marian Salzman

I can't remember very much about the senior prom, except that I wore a slinky black dress; that my date wore a baby blue rental tuxedo; and that somehow I persuaded my parents to let me give a pre-prom party that would take over the entire downstairs of our house, even though I wouldn't be there to participate in the clean-up effort.

The main items on the menu that night were "pigs in a blanket" — hot dogs wrapped in dough — and bite-size pizzas. We washed them down with sodas — my pre-prom party was "dry." That's right, despite the fact that we were about to be graduated from high school, our parents flexed their muscles, ranted and raved, and did everything but go along as flies on the wall to try to keep our alcohol consumption to a minimum. My parents, as our hosts, were the self-appointed wardens of Prohibition. As I remember it, the highlight of the party was when I sat, fully dressed, and helped to hem my date's trousers with a stapler.

The prom was held at a fancy restaurant, The Manor, in suburban West Orange, New Jersey. We sat at tables of five couples, and I, for one, have pictures to prove that none of us could quite understand what all the fuss was about. The thing I recall most clearly about the night was the constant confusion; I was something of a social butterfly, so I spent most of the prom working the floor — visiting acquaintances and friends and yakking up a storm, probably about nothing.

For some people, the senior prom is a big night, a once-in-a-lifetime, romantic event. For me, it was simply another party, perhaps more formal, but nothing to write home about. I think the prom bombed for me because I was already, on some level, living my postgraduation life, and I saw this ritual for what it was: an expensive night at a pretentious restaurant. Don't get me wrong. Part of me was into it. But I think the fact that the prom gets built up so much makes it a disappointment for a lot of kids.

Part of my problem with the prom was that I have never been much of a dancer. Forget the waltz — I can barely handle aerobics class, then or now. I was even a failure at the basic art of square dance, a required segment in physical education in my school district every year since elementary school. When it got more complicated than "Swing your partner and do-si-do," I zoned out. So the dance segment of the prom sort of bored me.

Most of the people in my prom picture had faded from my life by the time college graduation rolled around. I'm looking at a table photo right now. We all looked so fresh-faced, but it was obvious we were trying hard to be adults. I think we were anxious to grow up back then, as I'll bet all of you are now. That's the funny thing about high school — you spend four years dying to move beyond, but the minute you graduate, to college or a job, you begin to feel nostalgic about those incredible years.

Cliquety, Clique

"I think cliques are immature and for insecure people. We have a moderate amount of cliques at our school, but at smaller schools they are more apparent."

Mindy Povenmire, an eleventh grader at William Chrisman
High School in Independence, Missouri

Q & A: BUILDING A CIRCLE OF FRIENDS

Are all high schools cliquey?

Preps, jocks, skaters, burnouts, deadheads, granolas . . . the list goes on and on. Cliques have always been a part of the American High School Way. But are cliques a problem? A surprising number of you say no. "In my school there are groups of kids who seem to stick together, but there are no cliques that are antagonistic toward each other," says Dan Diman. But that's not always the case. Tracy Herman tells us that her high school is extremely cliquey. She deals with this by not sticking to one particular crowd and by having friends from pretty much every group in her school.

Those of you whose high schools are segregated by groups, don't despair. If you see cliques as barriers to popularity, or even friendships, you're better off just sticking to yourselves and being an "independent" until you naturally fall into groups of friends with whom you have something in common. Stephen,* a sophomore from Greenwich, Connecticut, tells us that his biggest mistake was leaping into a clique too soon and getting a reputation as being one of "them." It turned out in the long run that he really didn't want to be associated with that group, but he's had a hard time breaking off. His advice is to try to make friends one at a time rather than push right away for the security of a group.

Why do cliques form?

A common interest is usually what causes cliques to form, whether in junior high, high school, college, or life beyond school. By taking a look at a few of the most common cliques, we can see what it is that draws various people together.

The popular kids: It's not always looks; it's not always money; it's not always athletic ability. Kids tell us that the things that determine who's in the "in" crowd are really random. One trait they seem to share, though, is a sense of confidence. But keep this in mind: Kids in this clique also have dorky brothers and parents who dress like natives from the ozone layer.

The skaters: They love skateboarding, the outdoors, the California lifestyle. Depending on what part of the country you're from, the skaters could either be really "in" or they could be less desirable to hang out with than your little sister's Girl Scout troop.

The burnouts: Typically, the burnouts like to hang out in places where they can light up a butt — legally or illegally. But not all burnouts necessarily smoke cigarettes and listen to heavy metal. Some of them tend to be pretty philosophical and to read a lot of heavy stuff. Think of them as the Camus 'n' Camels crowd.

The "Oh-my-Godders": This clique is named after their favorite exclamation. You'll usually find them in the local mall or department store, trying new lipstick colors. Warning: High decibel levels likely.

The preps: You'll find them wherever you go. Docksiders, alligators, and upturned collars are out. These days, prepsters favor suede bucks, Polo shirts, and beefy all-cotton sweatshirts.

The jocks: The typical jock — crew-cutted, huge, and virtually illiterate — seems to transcend time. He's kept his image intact through the years. Remember Moose?

The dweebs: This group probably has the hardest time in high school, but they end up having the last laugh later in life when they go to prestigious colleges and get awesome jobs. It's never too late to invest in a scientific calculator.

What if I really want to get "in" with a certain clique but no one in it seems to like me?

The fact that you want to get into a clique should send up warning signals. Ask yourself why you want to be a part of this group. If it's to be popular, you're better off doing what you can as an individual to make yourself well liked. Certain cliques, especially the "desirable" ones, tend to be closed to outsiders. To be accepted, you'd probably have to alter something about yourself, whether it be the way you dress, the way you talk, whatever. But ask yourself this: Do you really want to be a clone? Are you sacrificing your individuality to become someone you're not? If what you really want is friends, become more involved in activities that interest you. It's a sure way to get to know people who like the things that you like.

The kids I hang out with have absolutely no interest in academics. Since I plan to go on to college, do you think I should try to get in with another group?

No one says you have to be a clone of your friends. The fact that your plans for the future are different from theirs doesn't make them any less valid. It's important for you to realize, though, that your friends may begin to resent it if you insist on informing them about every gory detail of your college application process. They shouldn't be expected to share your anxiety over every minor development. Just deal with the application on your own and continue to hang with them the rest of the time.

If, on the other hand, you think the influence your friends have on you is causing you to do poorly in school, you've got an entirely different problem. If your friends are pressuring you to blow off schoolwork and you usually give in, you're probably blaming them, consciously or unconsciously, for your academic difficulties. In this case, you're better off pulling away from them until you can get your own act together.

A lot of teens we've spoken to say it's helpful to have family rules to point to. Instead of hanging out watching videos every afternoon, tell your friends your parents are making you come straight home to do your work until your grades pick up. Ask your parents to back you up on this. After all, it's your life — there's no sense blowing your dreams just to get your friends off your back.

hs adviser

Moving Beyond a Clique

Advice from Donna Reed-Swihart, social worker, Burr Oak High School, Burr Oak, Michigan:

What can teenagers do to integrate themselves into their high schools and into their communities at large?

First, teenagers should not be told to integrate themselves with others. The desire to be part of the school community must come from within the student, although very often he or she may choose to remain uninvolved or alone.

Second, my best advice to a teenager is just to "be yourself." Don't conform to anyone else's philosophies, standards, or values. If you observe a student whom you admire and who you think has principles similar to your own, take a risk and reach out to that person. Communicate your desire for friendship. The worst that can happen is that he or she will not be receptive to you.

I believe that all systems in a community must function and operate with one another. One example of this cooperation is a community endeavor called Junior Achievement, in which individuals learn about the principles of business, the process of building trust, and the importance of teamwork. By developing and marketing consumer products as a team, the students gain a sense of accomplishment, pride, and trust in one another. Teenagers should be aware that it's okay to take risks and reach out.

Hollywood Yearbook: Can You Guess Which Cliques They Were In?

Burt Reynolds

Palm Beach High School '54

West Palm Beach, Florida

Activities: Football, Track, Key Club, Lettermen's Club, Student Council, Frond Staff, Basketball, B or Better Club.

Life's Goal: To be as well-liked as my father, and always have the friends I have now.

Geraldine Ferraro

Marymount High School '52

Tarrytown, New York

Activities: Newspaper Editor, Yearbook Editor, Debating Club, Glee Club, Field Hockey, Softball, Basketball. Voted Most Likely to Succeed. Career Goal: To be a newspaper reporter.

Tom Selleck

U.S. Grant High School '62

Van Nuys, California

Activity: Basketball.

Ellen (Jaclyn) Smith

Mirabeau B. Lamar Senior High School '64

Houston, Texas

Activities: National Thespian Society, Secretary '63; Modern Dance Club; Gym Leader.

Bruce Walter Willis

Penns Grove High School '73

Penns Grove, New Jersey

Activities: College Prep.; Student Council 1, 2, 3, Pres.; Percolator Blues: Harps; Junior Play. Life's Goal: To become deliriously happy or a professional harp player. **P**

Source: *Memories* magazine (August/September 1990)

What Was That Combination?

by Marian Salzman

The first room I could decorate as I truly wanted was the one I had to myself sophomore year at Brown. (You know the hassles we all face about inflicting our tastes upon our family homes. My mother's favorite lecture always began with, "While you're living in our home . . . .") It was exciting to decorate that not-very-modern, unfurnished attic room on Creighton Street in Providence, but I have to admit that though it was my first room of my own, it was not my first design project. Far from it. My first foray into interior decorating had taken place four years before. The project? My tenth-grade locker.

I still remember which wing of the high school my locker was on, and, if I really concentrate, I swear I'll be able to come up with the combination. All of the lockers at River Dell were that pasty brown color best described as that of day-old oatmeal. They were tall and narrow and had a shelf about three-quarters of the way up. The lockers were intended to be a place in which to store our books, coats, and after-school gear. In reality, we stocked them full of magazines to read in study hall; munchies to get us through lunch (since all the girls were dieting at least a quarter of the time); and various odds and ends without which we simply could not manage to get through the day — Frisbees, portable radios, umbrellas, extra pairs of shoes. . . .

The lockers became our sanctuaries — the one place where adult eyes never pried. We took these standard-issue boxes of metal and, by writing on them and in them, made them our own. We personalized them with photos of fab guys and of our friends. We cut funny sayings out of magazines and glued them to the inside of the door. The lockers even took on their owners' particular scents. Mine was redolent with the odors of Jontue and of American cheese and graham crackers — two staples of my teenage diet.

At River Dell, I'm pretty sure that our lockers were assigned by alphabetical order, the same as our homerooms were. Thus, my neighbor and comrade was my best friend, Fran, since her surname, Richardson, fell only slightly west, locker-wise, from mine. I can't seem to recall who was on my other side, but I have had a flash: One of the numbers of my combination was thirteen, and the second one was twenty-three. What was that third number?

I was lucky to have Fran next door to me. Having an obnoxious person at the next locker could be a real hassle. Two of my friends — Pete* and Doug* — got along fine as locker buddies until senior year. As college decisions started to trickle in, Pete decided that Doug was taking an unnatural (and thoroughly annoying) interest in Pete's acception-rejection stats. So Pete carefully concealed his rejections and let Doug steal glimpses of acceptance letters taped to the inside of Pete's locker door. What Pete hadn't reckoned on was that Doug would tell most of the

Class of 1977 that Pete was Princeton bound, when, in fact, the entire Ivy League had written him off and he was actually going to a school he considered "a lesser academic institution." It all worked out in the end, though. Today, Pete is quite the marketing executive, lesser academic institution and all. (Are you reading this, Doug?)

One of the great storage feats my locker performed sophomore year was the careful storing of a costume, including one of my father's smelly cigars, that I wore when I gave my oral report about the life of Francisco Franco, an important Spanish political figure. I decked myself out as if I were the man himself.

And then there was the time I found a flaky love note in my locker, from a boy who will go unnamed even here, since he was so shy and sincere in pledging his interest in me. Long before the days of personal ads and phone dates, American high school lockers served as an unofficial network of love. But they also served as fields of war.

I got into one of the nastiest confrontations of my life junior year with a senior who was waiting in front of my locker to tell me that she and her friends did not appreciate the fact that my friends and I were hanging out with boys they considered their property. She somehow had found out that the Brunettes had had a party with their guys the previous Friday evening, and she was boiling. I wish I could recall the specific threats she issued. Had any of them been acted upon, she might well still be in jail.

Whenever I visit high schools, I can't help but think fondly of those days when most things I needed were upstairs in my locker; when I was able to contact my nearest and dearest friends by leaving notes on their lockers. Now I lug around a briefcase that is distressingly empty of snacks whenever I want them, and I need to travel to different states, even continents, to visit with friends. It was so much easier being on two wings of River Dell Regional.

13

Money Matters

"Teenagers are very materialistic . . . it's society's addiction to money that has molded us."

Joey Williams, a twelfth grader at William Chrisman
High School in Independence, Missouri

Q & A: THE CASH CRUNCH

Clothes, concert tickets, CDs, stereos, cars, dating . . . everything costs so much money. How can I afford everything I want and need? And, if I can't afford it, how can I manage without it?

Competition for "stuff" in high schools, even in less-affluent inner-city schools, seems to have reached an all-time high. Kids today don't mind working part-time if it means having extra cash to spend on "luxury" items. If you do have an after-school job, you should be able to satisfy many of your material cravings. But not all teenagers are able to find work so easily, especially those of you who live in rural or suburban locations. And many of you who do find jobs say that they don't pay enough to get you through the month.

Obviously, a lot of you are attempting to support lifestyles that are neither possible nor necessary for the average teen to maintain. Unless your parents are extremely wealthy and ridiculously generous, you're going to have to find a way to bring your material goals back to reality. (And peer pressure doesn't necessarily have to dictate that designer goods and flashy electronic equipment are must-haves, even if that's what the folks on the boob tube are insisting.) Let's say you really want a pair of expensive sneakers. Aren't chances good that if you were to get them, they'd get kind of boring within a few weeks anyway? Test yourself by writing down on a slip of paper what it is you really want. Then look at it again in about a month. Do you still lust after it? Probably not. If you learn to distinguish impulse buying from spending money on things you *really* want and need, you'll end up with more money in your pocket and less stuff that sits unused in your closet or garage. "But half the thrill of getting stuff is saying you own it and were *able* to get bored with it," protests Christine Macbeth, an eighth grader at Garden City Middle School in Garden City, New York. She's right. But do you ever get bored with having money in your pocket?

My parents want me to concentrate on school, so they won't let me get a part-time job. How can I learn to manage money when all I get is an allowance?

Developing a healthy attitude about money while you're still in high school can really be to your advantage in the long run. A lot of kids get to college or begin a full-time job and have no idea how to write a check or balance a checkbook. Learning to manage money is something you should do when you're still at home so that you're able to ask your parents for help if you're not sure about something.

Even if the allowance you get is really minor, it might make sense to open a checking account. Some banks have no-fee accounts that are great for kids just starting out. In many cases, they don't even require a minimum initial deposit. Whenever you get your allowance, try to put at least some of it into your account. You'll be much less likely to fritter it away if you're forced to write checks even for minor purchases. Also, deposit any birthday or other special-occasion checks you get from relatives. You'll find they can really add up. Having a checking account will give you an entirely different attitude toward money. Even if you write only one check a month, you'll still be getting the hang of where your money is and where it's going.

My parents want me to give them the money I earn at my part-time job so that they can save it for me. How can I convince them to let me manage the $300 or so I earn each month?

Your parents might have some reason for thinking you're not responsible enough to handle your own money (i.e., they know you're going to spend it all). But since you're responsible enough to spend time and effort working after school and on weekends, it doesn't seem fair that you're not able to take charge of your earnings yourself.

Maybe you and your parents can reach some sort of compromise. If they're concerned about financing your college education, you should sit down and work out a plan whereby you'll save a certain portion of your income per month and have the rest to enjoy right now. You should also offer to pay for some of the things they're buying now — your car insurance, some of your clothes, and the like. You don't have to go overboard; just show them that you can handle money responsibly and that you are aware of your financial obligations.

David Portny recommends, "Work out a deal with your parents whereby you bank half your earnings for your future and get half your earnings to spend on things you want immediately. That way, you can decide how to spend half of what you make, and your parents have considerable input in how you spend the other half."

Credit-card companies are banging down my door offering "credit cards for kids." Does it make sense to start this early?

"Kids don't need credit cards," says Amanda Abraham. Resist the temptation. If you don't have enough money to buy something now, what makes you think you're going to have the money to pay for it at some point in the future? The companies want you to sign up for their credit cards because they make a lot of money from the fees and interest they charge you — money that could certainly be better spent elsewhere.

Credit-card companies may tell you that it's a good idea to start using credit now because doing so will help you in the future. But the truth is, as a teenager you're more apt to get into trouble with your credit card than you are to establish a good credit history. You'll have plenty of opportunities to get a credit card when you're in college or have started working full time. At that point, you'll be better able to judge how much you can safely charge to your credit card, and you'll be much more likely to be able to pay for those charges.

I love to shop. How can I spend my money wisely?

Most teenagers tell us that the phrase *saving money* just doesn't exist in their vocabulary. So, since you're going to spend it anyway, you might as well spend it on things that are going to be worthwhile. Don't buy things that are on sale just because they're on sale. Ask yourself if you would buy the item at its full price. If you wouldn't, you're looking at another potential money-wasting dust collector. Remember: It's better to have a few good things that you get a lot of use out of than a ton of cheap things that pile up in the back of your closet. When it comes to clothes and jewelry, the trendier the item, the less you're apt to wear it a year or even a couple of months from now. If you don't have that much money to throw around, stick with the basics and you won't go wrong.

It's also smart to be an informed consumer. If you're thinking of spending money on a large item such as a bicycle, make sure you don't just buy the first bike you see or the same one that your friends have. Take the time to look closely into the best-quality bikes. An easy way to do this is to look up the product in *Consumer Reports* or in an annual consumer guide, both usually available at local libraries. Most people agree that when it comes to major purchases, improved quality and durability are worth some extra money. (And will your parents ever be impressed by what a smart shopper you are! Translation: In the future, they may well give you even more freedom when it comes to managing and spending the money you earn, as well as your allowance.)

My parents are divorced and are constantly fighting about where I should go to college and who will pay my college tuition and expenses. I can't take it anymore. What should I do?

Even parents who are happily married can disagree about what kinds of financial obligations are appropriate for parents to assume in order to educate their children. The sooner you confront such matters, the better.

Schedule a family summit and set the agenda yourself. (If you need help identifying the issues that need to be resolved, meet with a trusted teacher or your guidance counselor or consult an older friend or relative who can be objective.) Once you have both your parents (and any concerned stepparent) in one room, talk to them about what's going on and ask if you can resolve the issues right then and there. If such a meeting is impossible to schedule, write your parents a letter that spells out exactly where you stand.

There are two important aspects of solving such a problem. The first is to figure out what each of your parents can realistically contribute toward your tuition, charges, and room and board. The second is to understand what each of your parents expects from the other in the name of fairness. If your mother expects your father to contribute an equal share and your father can't possibly afford that amount, consider asking your mother for a ten-year, no-interest loan to cover the difference between what your father is able to pay and what his equal share of the expenses would be.

Beth* was a junior at George Washington University when her father called to say that he would no longer be paying her full tuition and that she should ask her mother for a contribution. After many long-distance telephone calls to her father, in Lake Forest, Illinois, and to her mother, in Evanston, Illinois, Beth was forced to ask her maternal grandfather for help. "Luckily for me, he was able to lend me the $12,500 I needed to be able to finish school on time. I don't know what I would have done if Grandpa hadn't been able to swing the loan. I was devastated and even considered leaving school when I thought we — my mom and I — wouldn't be able to solve the problem."

Regardless of whether your parents are able to cover your college expenses, it makes sense to look into financial aid options. According to Brother David Van Hollebeke, associate director of admissions at Manhattan College, "The most common mistake families make is assuming that they are not qualified for financial aid. A number of factors determine who is eligible, not just family income." Brother Van Hollebeke recommends that students and parents check with high school guidance counselors about possible local scholarships. "And," he adds, "once parents receive a notice of financial aid from a college, they should go in person to the financial aid officer for possible readjustment. It pays to fight for more aid." If you can't get funding through institutional sources, consult your grandparents, aunts and uncles, older siblings, and godparents to see if they might be willing to assist you, either as guarantors of loans, as lenders, or even as benefactors.

hs adviser

Beyond the Piggy Bank

Vincent Appow of First Children's Bank in New York City talks about taking responsibility for your finances:

What advice do you give to kids about handling their money?
It is very important for young people to begin saving their money at as early an age as possible. I've seen youths in their early twenties who constantly bounce checks because they had never experienced financial responsibility at an earlier age. Along with learning how to write checks and balance their checkbooks, our customers at First Children's Bank have the responsibility of managing their own finances and choosing what to spend and what to save. These customers include kids as young as seven years of age who are proficient in check-writing, withdrawals, and deposits. Many of them have never bounced a check.

Who should consider opening an account?
Kids should open accounts only if they are aware of the responsibilities they will have and if they are planning to follow through and use the account on a regular basis. Don't open a checking account, write a few checks, then never make a withdrawal or a deposit again. It's very important that it be an ongoing process. Since our checking, savings, and college CDs are interest-bearing, you will see your money grow if you make deposits regularly.

Financial Aid Options for College

Financial aid packages may be funded by the federal or state government, commercial banks, colleges, or various other organizations that have been formed to help students in financial need. The following are the most common forms of aid.

Loans: Loans typically are repaid within a predetermined number of years after a student's graduation from college. There are a number of loan options available either through your chosen college or through federally sponsored programs. For information on Family Financing funded by Sallie Mae (Student Loan Marketing Association) call 1-800-831-LOAN. For information on loans for students whose families don't qualify for federal programs, call TERI (1-800-255-8374), Nelli Mae (New England Loan and Marketing) (1-800-634-9308), or ConSern Loan Program (1-800-767-5626). In addition, some banks provide loans to students: Citibank (1-800-828-6103), Manufacturers Hanover Trust (1-800-648-4723), and Bank of America (1-800-445-5488) are just a few.

Scholarships: Unlike loans, scholarships do not have to be repaid. There are more scholarships out there than you might imagine; unfortunately, many go unclaimed each year. A little research into scholarship sources can really pay off. Large companies often offer tuition assistance to employees and their children. Find out if your parents' companies offer aid programs for which you might be eligible. Or call The Foundation Center at 1-800-424-9836. For a small fee, they'll provide you with a computer printout of foundations that give tuition aid.

College Work-Study: This is a federally funded program that grants students the opportunity to earn money in order to help defray college expenses. Students generally work ten to twelve hours per week at campus jobs in food-service facilities, administrative offices, and so on.

For more information about financial aid and scholarships, consult *Peterson's College Money Handbook* and *Winning Money for College* (both Peterson's Guides; the former is published annually). [P]

Romance

"High school romance is a game — it's just a diversion from studying. But it makes high school a lot of fun."

Stacy Kinstlinger, a twelfth grader at Beachwood
High School, Beachwood, Ohio

Q & A: DATING DOS AND DON'TS

I'm usually pretty open with my parents, but I'm not sure whether to talk to them about my love interests. How much do you think I should tell them?

Some kids say, "Don't tell them *anything*." But that's not always the best advice. What you should choose to share with your parents may depend on a number of things. First, ask yourself what you're looking for from your parents. Do you want to use them as a sounding board, do you need their advice, or do you just want to keep them up to date on all of the important aspects of your life? If, as you say, you're usually fairly open with your parents, being totally secretive about this particular area of your life may damage that closeness between you. We're not suggesting that you share all the gory details, but you should at least let them know whom you're spending time with.

A second thing to consider is that, unjust as it may seem, many parents have a definite double standard when it comes to their kids' dating. Some parents accept their sons' girlfriends without question but attempt to run a full security check on any boy who comes within fifteen feet of their daughters. The best way to deal with this is to let your parents know where you stand on certain issues. Assure them that you're not some naive kid who is totally susceptible to all the horrible things that can befall teens these days. Parents are understandably worried about whether you'll be able to handle all the pressures you'll be confronted with as a teenager. Prove to them that you can take care of yourself, and they'll be much less likely to freak out whenever you mention a member of the opposite sex.

What are the advantages and disadvantages of dating someone exclusively?

"Dating" doesn't really seem to exist in high school anymore. When you hear the word, you probably think of teenagers back in 1957 going to drive-in movies, sipping malts at the local drugstore, and dancing cheek-to-cheek at the high school dance. These days, it's not uncommon to go through the entire four years of high school without a single traditional "date." Kids today pretty much either hang out in groups or have serious girlfriends or boyfriends. Emily Miller says that in her school "people don't really date randomly. If you go out with someone more than once, you're basically 'going out.'"

Teens we've spoken with have varying opinions about the pros and cons of "going steady." Meraiah Foley says, "If you're with one person all the time, you're missing out on a lot of other people with whom you could be doing things." But Meredyth Cohn, a sophomore at North Miami Beach Senior High School in North Miami Beach, Florida, tells us that "it's really nice to have that one guy to fall back on. It feels special to have someone who singled you out of the crowd and to know that it's just you two together."

Deciding whether to commit yourself to a relationship is probably not something you'll need to worry about. Either it will happen or it won't. Our advice is to curtail your freedom by having a serious boyfriend or girlfriend only if it's something you really want, not because your friends are doing it or because you'd like the security of a steady relationship.

How can I go about finding a date for a big event if there's no one in my life at that particular moment?

Here are a few suggestions from our co-authors:

•Gather your friends and go as a group. Many times you'll have more fun going as a "single" because you're not tied to any one person for the whole night.

•Ask someone from another town or school, maybe the son or daughter of a friend of your parents, someone you know from the summer, or a friend of a friend.

•If you're too shy to ask someone alone, ask a friend to join forces with you and approach two potential dates as a team. Make it a foursome . . . it'll be a blast.

If you've exhausted all of your resources and you refuse to go to the event on your own, don't sit at home moping about it. Make other plans. Take the money you would have used on the event and treat yourself and a friend to a nice dinner, a movie, or a play. You'll probably end up having a more enjoyable evening than you would have had at the event.

The other night, things got a little hot and heavy between me and my friend. She's a nice girl, but I want to remain "just friends." How can I tell her it was a mistake without hurting her feelings?

Fooling around with someone with whom you're "just friends" isn't a good idea, but if it happens, try not to feel guilty. It's almost as though there's some force of nature that drives platonic friends to step over the line at least once.

You should realize, however, that you're going to have to put in some extra effort to maintain the friendship and not let the inevitable barrier go up. If you feel uncomfortable around your friend, keep in mind that she must feel the same way and that not talking about it is just going to make it worse. Talk to your friend about what happened and let her know that you don't want to risk your friendship by turning it into something else. She may be disappointed, but the odds are good that she'll be as relieved as you are. Either way, you're both better off knowing where you stand.

I don't feel ready to be sexually active, and even if I did, I'd be scared about stuff like pregnancy and AIDS. How can I convince my friends this doesn't make me a loser?

You're right to be concerned about all the consequences of having sex.

102

It's not a decision to be made lightly, and it's something that can really mess you up — not just in terms of pregnancy or disease, but also in terms of coping emotionally with all of its related issues. If you don't want to be sexually active, the worst thing you could possibly do is let yourself be swayed by what your friends are doing or saying.

If your friends are pressuring you to have sex, ask them why they're so interested in your love life. Do you think that your teachers brag about sex to one another in the faculty lounge? That your parents ask their co-workers with whom they're fooling around? No! It's rude to pry into anyone's personal relationships, so don't feel pressured into explaining yourself to anyone.

My parents aren't prepared to talk with me about birth control. And I'm not thrilled with the idea of having to force a "birds and bees" conversation with them just because I need someone to advise me. Whom can I turn to?

Jeff Toohig notes that many parents prefer to pretend that their teenagers couldn't possibly be having sex. "A lot of kids I know are having sex or thinking about having sex," he says, "and they're not sure whom they can turn to for birth-control assistance because they don't want to upset their parents."

First and foremost, we can't stress enough that your decision to become sexually active should not be taken lightly. In talking to teens all over, it has become clear to us that many of you have made the decision to have sex. Unfortunately, many of you have made that decision without giving adequate thought to the possible consequences. Aside from the potential for emotional crises that arises when one engages in sexual activity before one is truly ready, there are the dangers of unwanted pregnancy, AIDS, and other sexually transmitted diseases (STDs). If you are sexually active, there is absolutely nothing that can protect you 100 percent from these dangers. By engaging in intercourse, you put yourself at risk — it's that simple.

If nothing you're taught can convince you to refrain from having sex, then the next best thing is to find out the best precautions to take. Again, there are no guarantees, but you can take certain steps that will afford you at least a degree of protection. Even if your parents are willing to talk with you about birth control and "safe" sex, you should ask them to make an appointment for you to speak with a professional. It's possible that your parents aren't aware of the latest findings and protections.

You should be aware, however, that there are resources teens can use for all services relating to health care and contraception. Once you begin having sex, you shouldn't be thinking only about contraception. Girls should be having regular Pap smears and gynecological checkups as well. Planned Parenthood, a national organization, provides a wide range of services that are confidential and free of charge to teenagers. Call 1-800-829-7732 for the center nearest you.

Francesca Canin, a social worker at Planned Parenthood in New York City, advises teens to find out whether their high schools have clinics, or to check the local Yellow Pages for hospital or family-planning clinics. "Most clinics, whether they are in your high school or in a hospital, provide services free of charge to teenagers," she says. So no matter where you're located in the country, a source of free, confidential services is probably just a few steps away.

If you have questions about your sexuality, Canin strongly recommends a book entitled *Changing Bodies, Changing Lives: A Book for Teens on Sex and Relationships*. This book was written by Ruth Bell with members of the Boston Women's Health Collective and published by Vintage Press in 1988.

What does "safe sex" mean?

Elizabeth Walters, a certified nurse–midwife associated with HITOPS (Health Interested Teens Own Program on Sexuality) in Princeton, New Jersey, says, "When we discuss unwanted pregnancy and sexually transmitted diseases with teens, we stress 'safer' sex guidelines rather than 'safe' sex because we all know that the only way to be absolutely safe is to abstain from sexual intercourse. We also discuss sexual behaviors such as kissing, holding, and touching, which are extremely low risk for pregnancy and STDs.

"For teens who have made a decision to have sexual intercourse, we recommend the three Safer Sex Guidelines outlined by Lynda Madaras in her book *Lynda Madaras Talks to Teens About AIDS:* (1) limit your partners, (2) know your partner, and (3) use condoms and spermicide every time you have intercourse. It is well known that the more partners a person has the more likely he or she is to contract an STD. It is also extremely important to know your partner's sexual history so that you can decide not to have sexual intercourse if that person has been engaging in high-risk behavior. We strongly urge both the male and the female to have their own method and to use it every time they have intercourse. He needs to use a condom; she needs to use a spermicide, sponge, and pills for maximum protection against both unwanted pregnancy and STDs."

hs adviser

Making the Right Choices

Here's what Dr. Nina Kaplan Singer, a New York therapist, tells teenagers about becoming sexually active:

What advice do you give to young people about sexual activity?
As a therapist who counsels many young people, I find it very unfortunate that sexual peer pressure is as strong as it is today. My experience leads me to believe that premature sexual activity has long-lasting negative effects. Women who began sexual relations at a very young age, or before they were really ready, often have low self-esteem and are convinced that the only thing they have to offer is their sexuality. And adult men sometimes feel guilty and depressed about their sexual activity as youths. As a teenager, your hormones are raging, and just because you "want to" isn't enough justification to commit yourself to sexual intercourse. Never offer your body before you offer your mind. The most vital thing to keep in mind is that you must use caution before you become intimate. With respect to sex, my advice to teenagers is simply, "Don't do it."

Whom can teenagers talk to about sex?
An open relationship with your parents about sex is very important psychologically. Although you don't necessarily have to agree with everything your parents tell you, it's important to listen to what they have to say and to allow them to offer you some guidance.

Are You Meant to Be a Swingin' Single or a Settled Steady?

1. **Your best friend breaks up with his or her steady and is rejoicing in the freedom. He or she has quickly become The Scam-Master. You feel:**
a. Like saying, "Scamming is really immature."
b. Like you want to join in on the fun, but that the fun won't involve flirting with anyone and everyone.
c. Like joining the party.

2. **You find out that your steady has been cheating on you. You:**
a. Burst into tears and contemplate becoming a monk or nun.
b. Confront him or her and try to reason it out.
c. Say "Screw it" and make the moves on everyone who comes near you.

3. **It's your boyfriend's or girlfriend's birthday. You:**
a. Spend a ton of money on presents and stay up all night baking a cake.
b. Get a reasonably priced present and write a nice card.
c. Contemplate breaking up so you won't have to fork over a gift.

4. **Your parents insist that you join them for a family vacation. Your steady is going to be leaving for boarding school during that time. You:**
a. Tell your parents that if they make you go, you'll whine incessantly for two weeks straight.
b. Suggest that your steady join you and your family — at least for a few days.
c. Are psyched that you'll be away and won't have to help your steady pack.

5. **Your older sister gets engaged and is totally thrilled. You:**
a. Ask her for tips on how she managed to pull it off.
b. Are happy for her but realize that everyone's time will come.
c. Buy her a ball and chain as an engagement present.

Scoring: Add up your points as follows:
a = 5
b = 3
c = 1

5–11 A Player of the Field
You're definitely not the "go steady" type. Relationships make you cringe, at least at this point in your life.

12–18 A Middle-of-the-Roader
Although you're not averse to romantic commitment, you're not actively seeking it either.

19–25 Committed to Commitment
You like to have that one person around who's as comfortable as your electric blanket. $\boxed{\text{P}}$

15

Sports, Fitness, and Health

**"I played soccer for most of my life and I loved it.
I want sports to always be a part of my life."**

Kevin Miller, a twelfth grader at Gainesville
High School in Gainesville, Florida

Q & A: FIT FOR FUN

What's more important: being a good sport or a winner?

Being a champion is an unbeatable feeling. Who wouldn't want to be the best at something? But when you look at the big picture, good sportsmanship is a quality that's going to last a lot longer than the shine on your trophies.

Being a good sport goes way beyond the playing fields. Throughout your life, you'll be faced with situations in which being fair and honest may cost you — but only in the short run. The decisions you're making now about the person you want to be will in large part determine how you handle yourself down the road. Honing your sportsmanlike skills while in high school will give you the edge you'll need to succeed.

How can I enjoy sports without feeling the pressures of competition and without feeling as though I have to win?

Many of you say that sports are a great way to get rid of stress. But some of you feel that sports are actually a big source of stress. "Just making it onto the varsity field hockey team was a giant pressure at the beginning of the school year," says Lisa Torrisi, a junior at Brooks School in North Andover, Massachusetts. Whether sports ease or cause stress for teens seems to be a matter of perspective. Those of you who play sports mostly because of the enjoyment you get from them say that you feel less pressure to win all the time. Your self-confidence doesn't seem to be tied to winning.

If you're not having fun on the playing field, take a moment to consider what it is you're getting out of your participation in sports. Jessica Berkeley tells us, "Sports really help me manage my time and help me feel as though I've got my schedule in order." Other benefits include staying in shape and meeting other students. Don't let your coach, your parents, or your teammates turn athletics into a chore for you. You should be playing for no one but yourself.

Is it normal to think that I'd be happier if I had a great body?

Unfortunately, yes. People of all ages seem to be under the impression that if they were to lose weight or pump iron, they'd be a lot happier, more popular, and more successful. Teenagers are particularly hit by feelings that they don't quite measure up, because adolescence is a time when kids increasingly compare themselves with their peers. And the majority of the time, they feel that they come up short. Okay, so some of us could stand to lose a few pounds or be more muscular . . . but that wouldn't change who we are. Our insecurities would just take a different form: We'd worry about our zits, our parents, or our lack of money.

If you ever really get down about your weight or appearance, consider why those things are so important to you. If you were stranded on a desert island, would you still be as upset about your looks? Probably not, because people most often worry about their appearance only in terms of what other people think. It's pretty lame to want to change your body just because you think then maybe you'd be accepted by certain people. If you want to be more attractive to others, work on your sense of self. A positive outlook and confident bearing will get you a lot farther than a perfect bod.

That's not to say, however, that having an exercise routine won't help you to feel better about yourself. Jeff Shammah, fitness expert and president of Total Fitness in New York City, claims that young people should seek the discipline instilled in them through exercising regularly. He says, "When you work for something, you learn the value of not getting something for nothing. Many kids today are unhappy with themselves, which results in self-destructive behavior such as using drugs and committing suicide. An exercise routine will help you to feel better about yourself because of its mental, physical, and spiritual effects."

School food isn't exactly low-calorie. What can I eat during the day to stay healthy, given the choices on the cafeteria line?

Many schools these days have a fix-it-yourself salad bar, which is definitely your best option if you're planning to buy lunch in the cafeteria. Just be sure to bypass the high-fat dressing. Nancy Wong says, "School food can be gross and sometimes it can be okay. The most important thing is to choose what you eat and to be flexible about your preferences." But who says you have to stick to cafeteria food? What's wrong with fixing your own lunch at home and brown-bagging it? If people rag on you, who cares? You'll be the one who's slim-and-trim and healthy while they're paying the consequences of scarfing down french fries and ice cream sandwiches.

If the consensus at your school is that the food stinks and that it's not good for you, do something about it. Tell the administration and food service people exactly what you do and don't like. As a last resort, organize a boycott or a walkout. It's important that kids have access to healthful foods, so don't back down. Your parents can also put pressure on the administration to improve lunchtime offerings. If you demonstrate the seriousness of your concerns, you'll most likely be able to get positive action — particularly if you make it clear to the administration that you're willing to pay a few pennies more for a decent and healthful meal.

I usually feel okay about my body, but when bathing-suit season rolls around, I want to be buried up to my neck in the sand. What can we beached whales do?

Very few Americans feel comfortable in a bathing suit. If we lived on a tropical island, it might be a different story, but in most parts of the United States we spend three-quarters of the year safely hidden under at least one layer of clothing. It's not easy to throw off our security blankets and reveal our palest secrets. So take solace in the fact that you're not alone.

Also keep in mind that if you're really and truly unhappy with the way you look in a bathing suit, you have the power to change your body through a fitness routine. So in a way you're lucky. Most physical features you don't care for, such as your height or the color of your eyes, can't be changed. But your physique and self-image can be altered dramatically through a little self-discipline. Take it into your own hands and see what a difference you can make before the next bathing-suit season rolls around.

How come some jocks have so much status in high school? You never see cross-country stars treated with the same fanfare as football, lacrosse, and soccer players.

The "sport of choice" at your school may depend on what your school excels in. Wilton High School in Wilton, Connecticut, for example, traditionally fields a very strong lacrosse team. So the lax players there may enjoy a higher standing than the football players. It's really a question of which sport has the strongest following.

Whether it concerns sports or after-school clubs or the cars teens drive, there will always be "in" things. These are the things that it is popular to do or own. In terms of sports, football is usually accorded the highest status in American high schools, perhaps because we're the only country that plays the game as we know it. It's an American trademark, so anyone who plays football is immediately considered an all-American guy. But don't assume that membership on a popular team automatically confers popularity. There are a lot of players who are cheered every Saturday when they take the field but who are just a face in the crowd come Monday morning. If you play a sport that's overshadowed by other sports at your high school, don't sweat it. As long as you're doing what you want to do, you're getting as much out of the sport as the kids on the high-profile teams.

High School Coaches on Sportsmanship

It's as important to be a good sport as it is to be a winner, say coaches nationwide.

"Don't underestimate the importance of acting in defeat as you would in victory. And when the game is over, congratulate the other team as you would want them to congratulate you. Don't harp on your losses." —Glenn Wyville, athletic director, Chagrin Falls High School, Chagrin Falls, Ohio

"Play as hard as you can play, but with common courtesies. There should never, ever be profanity or talking back on the field. Sports should come after the students' obligations to their parents, their education, and the school's staff." —Roy Walton, football coach, Tates Creek High School, Lexington, Kentucky

"Good sportsmanship is a very important aspect of life. In order to succeed in life, you are going to have to learn to deal with not only the wins, but the losses. Practicing good sportsmanship in high school will prepare you for what lies ahead." —Pam Monfort, field hockey/lacrosse coach, Manhasset Senior High School, Manhasset, New York

"Students must learn to keep an even keel on their emotions whether in victory or in defeat. Learn how to be a loser, not just a winner." —J.R. Holmes, boys' basketball coach, Bloomington High School, Bloomington, Indiana

"Play as hard as you can play, but make your supporters proud of your actions. They will be proud of you whether or not you win the game." —Dick Purdy, football coach, Lawrence High School, Lawrence, Kansas

A Personal Story About Bulimia

Teresa Reisgies talks about her first encounter with bulimia:

When I was in high school, one of my best friends, Lexie,* had bulimia for about eight months before anyone even suspected it. And we were a very close group of friends. We ate lunch together in the school cafeteria, spent practically every afternoon together, and slept at each other's houses on weekends. My other friends and I first got wind that something funny was up senior year, when, after a not-infrequent afternoon binge session of Oreos, peanut butter, and Jarlsberg cheese — fattening all — Lexie vanished into the bathroom for an extended period of time. That night, the girl whose house we were at discovered that someone had thrown up in the toilet, which hadn't been working properly.

Since we all knew that Lexie was very conscious of her weight and appearance, it wasn't very difficult to put two and two together and figure out that she was the culprit. After that initial incident, we looked back and remembered a lot of other little things that Lexie had been doing that left no doubt in our minds that she was bulimic.

At that point, we had to decide what to do next. None of us had the nerve to tell Lexie's parents, because we didn't want her to feel as though we were stabbing her in the back. At the same time, confronting Lexie was (we thought) useless because we knew she'd deny it. We spent about a week pondering our next move. Anyone we thought about spilling the beans to — the school nurse, a private doctor, a trusted teacher — came up short, because we knew that Lexie would be furious at us for embarrassing her.

Finally, Jill's* mom became involved because it was Jill's house where the toilet had stopped up. She wangled the information out of Jill and, before we knew

it, she had called Lexie's mom and told her everything. Lexie's mom confronted Lexie and made an appointment right away with a psychiatrist who specialized in eating disorders.

How did Lexie react? As expected, the denial factor kicked in right away. When she was forced to see the psychiatrist, she sat in with him but refused to say a word. She was furious at us, furious at Jill's mom, and basically furious at the world.

As it turned out, no shrinks or parents could make Lexie snap out of her bulimic behavior. It was a decision she had to reach on her own. Happily, she was able to overcome her eating disorder after her freshman year in college, by virtue of maturing and realizing what's really important in life. In retrospect, Lexie attributes her bulimia to the insecurity she felt when her high school boyfriend dumped her for a prettier, thinner girl. Lexie convinced herself that if she were thinner, her former boyfriend would want her back. In fact, it almost seemed to work. They did get back together briefly, which probably fueled Lexie's determination to lose more weight.

Now twenty-four and living in New York City, Lexie looks great, has a boyfriend who loves her just the way she is, and she can't imagine why she ever inflicted such damage on her body. "I couldn't have done anything more stupid," she says. "You can't go on being bulimic forever, and the more you do it, the more weight you're going to gain back when you finally stop.

It's a really stupid thing to do." Her advice to teens who think that being thinner will make their lives better: "It just doesn't work that way. You end up being much more miserable. Believe me — it's not worth it." [P]

The following organizations can provide information and referrals to self-help meetings for those with eating disorders:

American Anorexia/
Bulimia Association
133 Cedar Lane
Teaneck, NJ 07666
(201) 836-1800

Anorexics/Bulimics
Anonymous
4500 East Pacific Coast
Highway
Suite 330
Long Beach, CA 90804
(213) 597-7575

F.E.E.D. (Foundation for Education About Eating Disorders)
P.O. Box 34
Boring, MD 21020

Overeaters Anonymous
4025 Spencer Street
Suite 203
Torrance, CA 90503
(213) 542-8363

Food Addiction Hotline:
1-800-USA-0088

16

Summer Jobs and Volunteer Opportunities

"I love summer jobs because my parents make me pay for all my expenses and I get to earn the spending money I need during the summers. I really look forward to working every summer."

Rebecca Rieker, a ninth grader at Roncalli High School, Aberdeen, South Dakota

Q & A: MAKING THE MOST OF JUNE, JULY, AND AUGUST

What's better for the summer: play or work?

Many high school students enjoy vegging out over the summer. Jessica Berkeley tells us, "Having free time to relax and do whatever I want during the summer is really important to me." But this doesn't necessarily mean that students want to be completely unproductive for three months. Jessica, for example, is planning to spend half the summer hanging back and the rest of the summer working in an underdeveloped country. Some of the programs that send teens to work overseas sound really neat, but there's usually one problem: They cost money, even though you're going there to work. The program that Jessica's considering costs $2,000 — not cheap!

Staying at home and working to earn money for the school year is a good alternative, especially if you can find a "fun" job that allows you to combine the best of both worlds. Colin Robinson, an eighth grader at Garden City Middle School in Garden City, New York, cuts lawns for his neighbors on weekends, which gives him a lot of flexibility. A job at a place in which a lot of your friends hang out, like the beach, the pool, or the local pizzeria, lets you stay on top of the action while earning your paycheck. Or what about volunteering for a local company in an industry that you think you might want to get into in the future?

I want to spend next summer in a recreational setting. Is there any way I can do that and earn money at the same time?

Your best bet is to work as a counselor at a camp that specializes in outdoor activities. Attend camp fairs sponsored by the American Camping Association to find out the names and specialties of the hundreds of camps out there. Or, if you already have a camp in mind, contact the director a few months in advance and express your interest in employment.

Another great way to enjoy the outdoors while earning money is to work in a national park or in a hut run by the Appalachian Mountain Club. The AMC huts offer overnight lodging and meals to hikers on the Appalachian Trail. Imagine living on top of a mountain for the summer. Or, consider working at a dude ranch in the Rocky Mountains or along the west coast. These ranches offer plenty of employment opportunities and almost always provide room and board.

If you'd prefer a recreational setting that's not quite so rugged, consider working at a theme park or summer resort. These places rely heavily on seasonal workers, and you're sure to have lots of fellow employees your age to hang out with.

I know volunteer work looks great on college applications and resumés, but I need to make money. How can I make a nonglamorous job look good on my permanent record?

Lots of high school students complain that the "best" internships and "do-gooder" jobs are usually nonpaying. But don't think that working at a regular job will carry any less weight with admissions committees and potential employers. Any job, even if it's flipping burgers at your local fast food joint, will look good on your record. What you should do to make the most of the experience is get a letter of recommendation from your manager. Ideally, the letter should stress your commitment to the job, your hard work and fantastic interpersonal skills, and the contribution you made to the business. If you're applying to college, you'll also score points if you can show that you spent your salary in a responsible way. Let admissions officers know if you bought your own car or if you contributed to the family income.

If you'd still prefer to have something a little more eye-catching on your record, keep in mind that volunteer work doesn't have to be full time. If you have the time and inclination to help out somewhere after work, try to squeeze it in. It will still look good on your record, and, more important, you'll be providing a helping hand to someone who really could use one.

How can I go about getting a good summer job?

First of all, let everyone know that you're in the market for a summer job. Have your parents tell their friends, have your friends tell their parents, tell your teachers and counselors at school. Also, scan the want ads in the papers and call the manager or personnel office of any organization or business in which you're interested. A lot of companies and businesses really count on summer help from high school kids. If you really want to work at a particular place, but the employers aren't willing to fork over a salary, try volunteering on a week-to-week basis. After a few weeks, they might really need you and offer to put you on salary. If nothing else, you'll get great experience and be in a better position to land a job the following summer.

When looking for a summer job, it's always a good idea to have at least two letters of recommendation from teachers at school or from previous employers. Make photocopies and attach them to every job application you fill out, even if recommendations are not requested. If a potential employer seems hesitant to hire you because you're going to be only summer help, tell him or her that you'd consider working part time after school in the fall. If your youth seems to be an obstacle, point out that your young age makes you more energetic, flexible, and willing to work harder to prove yourself. Learning how to toot your own horn is the trick to getting a great summer job.

Trailblazer

Interview with Laurie Peele, a graduate of Yorktown High School in Arlington, Virginia, who participated in a summer program of the Appalachian Trail Conference:

What did you actually do on the Appalachian Trail?
Our trail crews were the elite of the Appalachian Trail. The work mostly entailed heavy-duty trail repair, digging side trails, moving heavy boulders, and building bridges. We used a wide range of tools, all of which were carried by us. And, although no prior experience was required, the work was extremely physically demanding.

Who was in your group?
Everyone from high school and college students to retirees . . . from the educated to the non-educated, the old to the young. But, overall, I would say there were more young people, of high school and college age.

What was the best thing about your experience?
We all left with a great sense of camaraderie and accomplishment. We had worked together with team spirit and a sense of doing something constructive and worthwhile. It's really rewarding to have such a tangible result at the end of the week — we could actually see what we had accomplished.

Did the program cost money?
There are no prerequisites or fees for joining this program, and everyone receives a small stipend. However, since the applicant pool is growing in number, the program is becoming more competitive.

For more information, contact: Appalachian Trail Conference; P.O. Box 807, SOT-1; Harpers Ferry, WV 25425; (304) 535-6331.

Twenty Summer Jobs You Can Find in Your Own Community

☆ Day-camp counselor

☆ Instructor in something you're good at: tennis, football, swimming

☆ Aide to elderly or physically challenged person(s)

☆ Day-care-center assistant

☆ Lifeguard

☆ Park Service assistant

☆ Candy striper at hospital (volunteer)

☆ Mother's helper

☆ Retail salesperson

☆ Waiter/waitress

☆ Kitchen assistant

☆ Tutor

☆ Office assistant (possibly in mom's or dad's office)

☆ Concession stand worker

☆ Library clerk

☆ Sunday School teacher

☆ Lawn-care worker

☆ Domestic helper/odd jobs

☆ Entrepreneur — start your own business

☆ Intern in a company, organization, or local government office P

17

Summer Adventures

"Summer, to me, is for adventure. The biggest adventure I can imagine would be to explore Australia."

Mandy Williams, an eleventh grader at Grapevine High School in Grapevine, Texas

Q & A: EXPERIENCES OF A LIFETIME

Is there an inexpensive way to go abroad for the summer?

Absolutely. Just think about it for a minute. Kids in most foreign countries hear such great things about America, and the hottest items around are American blue jeans, rock music, and name-brand sneakers. Don't you think there are tons of kids over there who are just dying to come to the States for a couple of weeks? So why not set up your own mini-exchange?

Start off by choosing the country to which you'd like to go. Go to the library and do some thorough research, using guidebooks, travel magazines, and any other sources available to you. Once you've chosen a particular spot in a country, get the names of as many schools as possible in that region. For example, if you decide on Germany and you want to be in

Frankfurt, find out the names and addresses of some of the city and suburban schools there. If you're having trouble finding this information, you might want to get help from a local high school or college foreign-language department. They may have contacts in that part of the world. Or, call or write that country's embassy in Washington, D.C.

Once you have the info, send a letter to the heads of the schools in which you're interested. If you're proficient in the foreign language or know someone who can help you draft a letter, that's great. If not, don't worry about it — a letter in English will more than likely be understood. Express your desire to set up an exchange with a student in the school. Say that you'd be willing to house this student for half of the summer or during any vacation time in return for your being able to stay with him or her for an equal amount of time next summer. Include as much information about yourself as you can, stating clearly why it is that you're interested in the particular country and region you've chosen. If it matters to you, be clear about whether you want your exchange partner to be a girl or boy and state minimum and maximum ages. You should of course consult your parents while you're making these plans, as trading places involves your entire family. And, if your father, or mother, or both, are reluctant for you to enter into such an arrangement, find other families who have hosted exchange students, or whose teenagers have traveled abroad, and ask them to help you make a list of the pros of student exchanges. Your parents may just need some convincing.

Writing to schools abroad will usually work if you send out a good number of letters at least four or five months before you're planning to travel. Then all you're going to have to pay for is plane fare and spending money. Depending on the time of year, you may even be able to get a substantial student discount on your plane ticket. A travel agent may be able to book you on a charter flight that costs as little as $500 round-trip.

What's an ideal summer for high school kids?

"A summer with no parents and no summer reading." —Daniel Folmar, Indian Springs School, Pelham, Alabama

"A road trip out West in an open vehicle, hiking through the deserts and parks." —Kathryn Alexander, Bearden High School, Knoxville, Tennessee

"Working in a research lab to find a cure for AIDS or cancer." —Andrew Hunter, Groton School, Groton, Massachusetts

"Exploring the Australian Outback." —Paul Campbell, Brookland Cayce High School, Columbia, South Carolina

"Going to snowboarding camp in Oregon." —Kirk Kenfield, Portsmouth Middle School, Portsmouth, Rhode Island

"A West Coast Teen Tour combined with visits to all of the colleges on the west coast." —Meredyth Cohn, North Miami Beach Senior High School, North Miami Beach, Florida

"Starring in an action-comedy movie being filmed on location." —Brian Klugman, Germantown Academy, Fort Washington, Pennsylvania

"Being a counselor at a camp — dealing with children, teaching, swimming, and having a lot of responsibility." —Leigh Danforth, Cranbrook Kingswood School, Bloomfield Hills, Michigan

How can I figure out what would make an ideal summer for me?

There are so many options out there that it really helps to narrow down your focus before you start making plans. Ask yourself the following questions:

- Do I want to earn money or volunteer?
- If I'm considering a program that costs money, how much do I want to spend?
- Do I want to stay in the United States or go abroad?
- If I'm considering a job, do I want to work with people my own age or get a taste of the business world?
- Do I want to be in a structured environment or do my own thing?
- Do I want to be in a leadership position, or do I prefer to follow?
- Do I want to travel or be in the same place all summer?
- Do I want to be physically challenged?
- Do I want to do something that would look good on my college or job applications?
- Do I want to be in a single-sex environment?
- Do I want to improve a specific skill?
- How much free time do I want?

If my parents don't want to host an exchange student, what are my best low-cost options for programs abroad?

•Volunteer service: Although some volunteer organizations require payment from participants, others ask only that you pay the cost of your transportation to and from the volunteer site. More often than not, your food and lodging will be the only "freebies" you'll get in return. But don't automatically write off programs that require payment. You might be able to secure substantial financial aid.

•Paid internships: Believe it or not, they do exist, although they may require that you speak a foreign language. In most cases, you'll be required to pay only for transportation.

•Homestays: Since travel and spending money could cost you $1,000 or more, homestays aren't cheap, but they sure beat paying for room and board in a hotel or youth hostel. Homestays involve living as a guest in people's homes. Thus, be prepared to be on your best behavior, since, on some levels, you're functioning as an American ambassador as well as a guest.

How tough is it to get into these programs?

The selectivity of summer programs obviously depends on the size and caliber of the applicant pool, but keep the following things in mind:

•Find out your chances of admittance well in advance. If you understand fully that you're applying to a competitive program, you'll be better prepared to make alternative plans should your first choice not pan out.

•If you're planning to attend an academic summer program, all of the pieces of your application (e.g., standardized test results, transcripts, and letters of recommendation) must be sent in on time. Make sure you understand the term *rolling admissions*. It means that applicants are considered on a first-come, first-served basis. So the earlier you get your application in, the better your chance of being accepted.

Australian Adventure

Interview with Peter O'Reilly, who spent the summer after his junior year at Groton School in Groton, Massachusetts, playing organized baseball in Australia:

How did you become involved with the organization that sent you abroad?

I heard about "Sport," which is affiliated with Youth for Understanding, through friends of my parents. Sports for Understanding sends groups of American kids to about twenty different countries to play various sports with those nations' native teams. So I filled out an application and listed three choices of what I'd want to do. It was, in order, to play baseball in Australia, soccer in Scotland, or baseball in Mexico. For the application, I needed a recommendation from my high school coach, proof that I had been playing the sport for a certain number of years, and a recommendation from a high school teacher or counselor, sort of just to show that I wasn't a troublemaker and that I could handle myself in a foreign country. I landed my first choice — baseball in Australia — and I was really psyched.

What did you actually do there?

I was with a group of fifteen kids from all around the country — actually, most of them were from the Midwest — and we had a coach who was a successful high school baseball coach in the U.S. For five weeks, we played baseball against Australian teams from all different parts of that country. We won all of our games. There was also enough free time to go sightseeing all over Australia. We spent a week in the Outback, which was great.

How much did it cost?

"Sport" paid for our airfare from Los Angeles to Adelaide, which was very substantial. We had a program fee, which wasn't that much, and then spending money. We stayed with families, so there were no living expenses.

What was it like to live with an Australian family?
It was great. I didn't have any problems with my family. They were really supportive and came to watch all of our games. My "house mother" was pretty liberal about letting us go out at night. There weren't all that many cultural differences, other than the food, which was a little different from what we're used to, and some of the words they use. But some of my friends had families who weren't as willing to let them do what they wanted with their free time, which caused some problems. But, overall, I had a great experience and would do it again anytime.

For information, contact:

Sports for Understanding International Exchange
Department W
3501 Newark Street, N.W.
Washington, DC 20016-3167
1-800-424-3691

Ten Programs Worth Considering

Visions

Coed residential program focused on community service, construction, leadership training

Cost: $1,400 to $3,000 (financial aid available)

Contact: Mel Bornstein, Director

RD #3, Box 106A

Newport, PA 17074

(717) 567-7313

Earthwatch

Anthropological and other research work abroad

Cost: $800 to $2,400 (scholarships and fellowships available)

Contact: Brian Rosborough

680 Mount Auburn Street, Box 403

Watertown, MA 02272

(617) 926-8200

AMIGOS de las Americas

Community service volunteers in Central and South America

Cost: $2,020 to $2,400 (financial aid available)

Contact: Director of Admis-

sions, Community Service Volunteers

AMIGOS de las Americas

5618 Star Lane

Houston, TX 77057

(713) 782-5290

The Quebec Labrador Foundation

Internships in environmental education, water safety, and swimming

Cost: Only cost is travel to headquarters; stipend paid to volunteers

Contact: Director of Intern Operations

Atlantic Center for the Environment

Quebec Labrador Foundation

39 South Main Street

Ipswich, MA 01938-2330

(508) 356-0038

Habitat for Humanity International

Christian organization dedicated to building alternatives to poverty housing

Cost: None

Contact: Millard Fuller

Habitat and Church Streets

Americus, GA 31709

(912) 924-6935

Volunteers for Peace

International volunteer work camps

Cost: $80 per work camp

Contact: Volunteers for Peace

43 Tiffany Road

Belmont, VT 05730

(802) 259-2759

World Horizons International, Inc.

Summer volunteer programs worldwide

Cost: $2,500

Contact: World Horizons International, Inc.

1427 Second Avenue

New York, NY 10021

(212) 439-6292

Appalachian Mountain Club

Volunteer trail-maintenance programs in the United States and the Soviet Union

Cost: $20 to $125

Contact: Appalachian

Mountain Club
Trails Program
P.O. Box 298
Gorham, NH 03581
(603) 466-2721

CY-Tag
(Challenged for Youth—Talented and Gifted) Program focusing on academic enrichment
Cost: $790
Contact: CY-Tag
W171 Lagomarcino Hall
Iowa State University
Ames, Iowa 60011-3180
(515) 294-1772

London Summer Internships and Summer School
Residential program focusing on communications, government, law, business, and the arts.
Cost: $4700 to $4900 (financial aid available)
Contact: London Summer Internships and Summer School
Janet Kollek Evans, Director
158 West 81st Street, Box 112
New York, NY 10024
(212) 724-0804

For further information on summer opportunities: *Peterson's Summer Opportunities for Kids and Teenagers* (Peterson's Guides, published annually) or *The 1991 Guide to Accredited Camps* (American Camping Association, 1991), available from:
American Camping Association
5000 State Road, 67 North
Martinsville, Indiana 46151 P

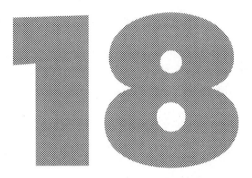

The Media

"I watch a lot of television news and think that the information given out is fine — enough for our purposes. But sometimes it's a little bit filled with propaganda intended to keep our spirits up."

Kristin Kirkman, a twelfth grader at Greensboro Day School in Greensboro, North Carolina

Q & A: STRAIGHT FROM THE SOURCE

I'm a current affairs buff. What newspapers and magazines should I read to be sure that I'm fully informed?

Current affairs teachers from both public and private schools around the country advise students to read at least one national news magazine per week, as well as a daily newspaper from the city closest to them. To give you an idea of what other students are reading, we talked to current affairs students in Indiana and California. At Carmel High School in Carmel, Indiana, students are advised to read the *Indianapolis Star*, the *Indianapolis News*, and either *Time* or *Newsweek*. Students at

Huntington Beach High School in Huntington Beach, California, are advised to read the *Los Angeles Times*, the *Orange County Register*, and either *U.S. News & World Report* or *Time*. Reading, or at least skimming, publications such as these will keep you up to date on the latest happenings in the nation and the world.

You also should watch the national news on television — but be aware that news producers are inundated with stories to cover and, as a result, may touch only briefly on issues of importance to you. Use television news as a supplemental news source only, not as your mainstay. Other shows to consider: "Meet the Press," "This Week with David Brinkley," "Week in Review," and "Nightline," although we recommend that you tape the latter if you're planning to be awake in your morning classes. And there are a number of prime-time news shows that offer magazine-style reports; many of these are worth catching.

Why have some "news" programs become so sensational?

Many people deny that they watch shows like "A Current Affair" and "Inside Edition." But, let's face it, someone must be watching or their ratings wouldn't be so good. It seems that many of us have a strange sense of curiosity when it comes to learning the gory details about crime, violence, deceit, and celebrity mishaps. As soon as one show crosses the invisible line of discretion and succeeds, others start to follow suit. The networks may like to brag about their quality programming, but if they can make more money on gossip and gore, they'll go for it.

One producer told us that programming competition has become very personal. If a show's ratings aren't considered high enough, the producer could very well get the ax. The next producer hired will be told, right off the bat, that he or she must improve the ratings or suffer the same fate. When faced with this kind of pressure, it's no wonder producers sometimes try to make the news more exciting than it actually is.

I've never been much of a reader, but sometimes I wish I were. What can I do to motivate myself to pick up a book once in a while?

Even those of you who claim you don't like to read say there are certain books you like. Examples of these? *Catcher in the Rye, At Risk*, and *The Outsiders*. So maybe it's not that you don't like reading. It could be that you just haven't enjoyed a lot of the books you've been required to read in school. Try reading books about things you really enjoy, such as your hobbies and special interests. Say, for example, you like music. If so, try

Chartbreaker, by Gillian Cross (Holiday, 1987). In it, a seventeen-year-old high school student who sings part time with a rock group faces family problems as a result of her musical aspirations. Or, if you're interested in outdoor life and travel, read *Iron and Silk*, by Mark Salzman (Random House, 1987), which is the firsthand tale of an American's experiences teaching English in China. Finally, if you like sports and recreation, read *Running Loose*, by Chris Crutcher (Dell, 1986), in which a teenager is psyched to begin his senior year in high school — he's a starter on the football team and is going out with the girl of his dreams. But life isn't so rosy when he's thrown off the team and his girlfriend dies in a car accident.

I hear that some college interviewers ask what books students have most enjoyed. Is there a "right" answer to this question?

It's important that you've read some "core" books that college admissions officers think all high school students should have read by the time their senior year rolls around. (See this chapter's FYI for an idea of what some of these books are.)

But what the admissions officers are probably wondering is whether and what you like to read. If you've read a lot of books on a particular topic, tell your interviewer about it. Impress him or her with your intellectual curiosity. It's not necessary to fake a lifelong interest in the Greek classics; anything from modern American short stories to science fiction will do. We recommend that you keep your taste for romance novels to yourself, though (unless, of course, the interviewer has a framed poster of Barbara Cartland on the wall).

If the admissions officer asks your opinion of a particular classic, it's not necessary to rave about it. But don't say you didn't like it unless you can cite intelligent reasons. Otherwise, you run the risk of sounding as though you didn't put enough energy into reading the book.

To what magazines do teens typically subscribe?

Some of our female co-authors' favorite magazines are:

Cosmopolitan	*People*	*Time*
Elle	*Sassy*	*ym*
Glamour	*Seventeen*	
Mademoiselle	*Teen*	

Our male co-authors say they enjoy:

Baseball Digest	*Newsweek*	*Surfer*
Basketball	*Snow Country*	*Teen and*
Inside Hockey	*Sports*	*Gymnastics USA*
Mad	*Sports Illustrated*	*Tennis*
National	(the overwhelming	
Geographic	favorite)	

Boob Tubular

Interview with Harris Salomon, producer, HA! Channel:

What makes a TV show "hot"?
Coming up with a new TV show is like reinventing the wheel. It's all the same stuff, over and over again, but done differently. So what makes it hot is very arbitrary. Often, it's nothing more than the fact that the show is, quite simply, good television. What's good television? Something that's interesting, creative, and well done — shows such as "thirtysomething" and "L.A. Law." At the same time, sometimes shows that are expected to be hits don't catch on. "St. Elsewhere" had terrible ratings when it first started to run, but someone at the network had the foresight to realize that the show would eventually pick up because it was quality television.

On the other hand, shows such as "The Simpsons" are hot for no explainable reason. People start talking about them, and all of a sudden everyone wants to watch. Shows such as these are more trendy, however, and will tend to have much less staying power.

What can TV do for me?
First, TV is a tool for communication that has changed our culture and will continue to do so. In a few years most of us will have access to global television; we will watch programs from around the world.

Second and more important, we have found that television has the power to make people feel good and laugh, which is a pretty big accomplishment these days. Stupid as it may sound, people laugh when they see someone slipping on a banana peel. It's sort of a piece of human nature. If we can bring that laughter into your life, then we're doing our jobs right.

Reading List *

(ORGANIZED ALPHABETICALLY, BY TITLE)

Ninth Grade:

Frankenstein, by Mary Shelley

Go Ask Alice, Anonymous

The Heart Is a Lonely Hunter, by Carson McCullers

The Hollow Hills, by Mary Stewart

The Human Comedy, by William Saroyan

The Iliad, by Homer

The Illustrated Man, by Ray Bradbury

Jane Eyre, by Charlotte Brontë

Jason and Medea, by John Gardner

Julius Caesar, by William Shakespeare

The King Must Die, by Mary Renault

Myths and Folklore, by Henry Christ

The Natural, by Bernard Malamud

Of Mice and Men, by John Steinbeck

On the Beach, by Nevil Shute

The Once and Future King, by T. H. White

The Outsiders, by S. E. Hinton

Pudd'nhead Wilson, by Mark Twain

A Raisin in the Sun, by Lorraine Hansberry

Red Sky at Morning, by Richard Bradford

R Is for Rocket, by Ray Bradbury

Silas Marner, by George Eliot

S Is for Space, by Ray Bradbury

Turn of the Screw, by Henry James

Where the Lilies Bloom, by Vera and Bill Cleaver

You Can't Take It with You, by Moss Hart and George Kaufman

* Provided by the National Council of Teachers of English.

Tenth Grade:

A Separate Peace, by John Knowles

Adventures of Huckleberry Finn, by Mark Twain

All Quiet on the Western Front, by Erich Maria Remarque

Autobiography of Miss Jane Pittman, by Ernest Gaines

Beloved, by Toni Morrison

Canterbury Tales, by Geoffrey Chaucer

Catcher in the Rye, by J. D. Salinger

Cat's Cradle, by Kurt Vonnegut

The Color Purple, by Alice Walker

The Crucible, by Henry Miller

Death of a Salesman, by Arthur Miller

Don't Play Dead Until You Have To, by Maia Wojciechowska

The Effect of Gamma Rays on Man-in-the-Moon Marigolds, by Paul Zindel

The Good Earth, by Pearl S. Buck

The Grapes of Wrath, by John Steinbeck

The Great Gatsby, by F. Scott Fitzgerald

Grendel, by John Gardner Jr.

Hamlet, by William Shakespeare

I Know Why the Caged Bird Sings, by Maya Angelou

Ironweed, by William Kennedy

Mama Day, by Gloria Naylor

A Man for All Seasons, by Robert Holt

Master Harold and the Boys, by Athol Fugard

A Midsummer Night's Dream, by William Shakespeare

One Day in the Life of Ivan Denisovich, by Aleksandr Solzhenitsyn

The Red Badge of Courage, by Stephen Crane

Roll of Thunder, Hear My Cry, by Mildred Taylor

Romeo and Juliet, by William Shakespeare

The Scarlet Letter, by Nathaniel Hawthorne

Stranger in a Strange Land, by Robert A. Heinlein

Their Eyes Were Watching God, by Zora Hurston

The Unvanquished, by William Faulkner

Weep Not, Child, by James Ngugi

Winesburg, Ohio, by Sherwood Anderson

Working, by Studs Terkel

Eleventh Grade:

...And Ladies of the Club, by Helen Hooven Santmeyer

As I Lay Dying, by William Faulkner

The Bear, by William Faulkner

A Bend in the River, by V. S. Naipaul

The Bluest Eye, by Toni Morrison

David Copperfield, by Charles Dickens

Dinner at the Homesick Restaurant, by Anne Tyler

A Doll's House, by Henrik Ibsen

Elements of Style, by William Strunk and E. B. White

A Farewell to Arms, by Ernest Hemingway

The Hobbit, by J. R. R. Tolkien

In Our Time, by Ernest Hemingway

Lord Jim, by Joseph Conrad

Losing Battles, by Eudora Welty

The Mayor of Casterbridge, by Thomas Hardy

Midaq Alley, by Naguib Mahfouz

Miramar, by Naguib Mahfouz

My Antonia, by Willa Cather

Of Human Bondage, by Somerset Maugham

Out of India, by Ruth Prawer Jhabvala

A Passage to India, by E. M. Forster

The Power and the Glory, by Graham Greene

Pride and Prejudice, by Jane Austen

The Prime of Miss Jean Brodie, by Muriel Spark

Rich in Love, by William Humphreys

Sister Carrie, by Theodore Dreiser

The Street, by Ann Petry

The Thief and the Dogs, by Naguib Mahfouz

Tom Jones, by Henry Fielding

2001: A Space Odyssey, by Arthur C. Clarke

Wuthering Heights, by Emily Brontë

Twelfth Grade:

Absalom, Absalom!, by William Faulkner

The Age of Innocence, by Edith Wharton

All the King's Men, by Robert Penn Warren

Anna Karenina, by Leo Tolstoy

The Awakening, by Kate Chopin

Crime and Punishment, by Fyodor Dostoyevsky

Cry, the Beloved Country, by Alan Paton

Dr. Faustus, by Christopher Marlow

Ethan Frome, by Edith Wharton

Fathers and Sons, by Ivan Turgenev

Go Tell It on the Mountain, by James Baldwin

The Grass Harp, by Truman Capote

Gulliver's Travels, by Jonathan Swift

The Hamlet, by William Faulkner

A Handful of Dust, by Evelyn Waugh

Hedda Gabler, by Henrik Ibsen

Invisible Man, by Ralph Ellison

Leaves of Grass, by Walt Whitman

Light in August, by William Faulkner

Lord Jim, by Joseph Conrad

Moby Dick, by Herman Melville
Native Son, by Richard Wright
1984, by George Orwell
One Hundred Years of Solitude,
  by Gabriel García Márquez
The Portrait of a Lady, by Henry James
A Portrait of the Artist as a Young Man,
  by James Joyce
Rabbit, Run, by John Updike
The Return of the Native, by Thomas Hardy
A Room of One's Own, by Virginia Woolf
The Russians, by Hedrick Smith

Since Yesterday, by F. L. Allen
Slaughterhouse-Five, by Kurt Vonnegut
Song of Solomon, by Toni Morrison
Sons and Lovers, by D. H. Lawrence
The Sound and the Fury, by
  William Faulkner
The Sound of Waves, by Yukio Mishima
Sula, by Toni Morrison
The Tempest, by William Shakespeare
Three Plays, by Edward Albee
To the Lighthouse, by Virgina Woolf
Waiting for Godot, by Samuel Beckett [P]

19

We Are the World

"Due to our growing population, if I could go anywhere in the 'world,' I would go to space to make it habitable for mankind."

Andy Bush, an eleventh grader at Abbeville
High School in Abbeville, Alabama

Q & A: IT'S A SMALL WORLD AFTER ALL

Should I take my school's community service requirement seriously? If so, how do I know what kind of project is best for me?

Chris Pennisi, an eleventh grader at Manhasset High School in Manhasset, New York, advises: "If you have to do community service for a school requirement, look deep within yourself and do some soul searching. Decide, 'Who am I doing volunteer work for?' Many people join clubs and sign up for community service just because they have to or they want a college recommendation or they are competing for a scholarship. I think that's where many kids miss the concept of community service.

Anything you can do to help out someone other than yourself is more valuable than you can imagine. And even though you may be busy, make the largest commitment that you possibly can because the more you put in, the more you will get out of volunteering. Once you develop a great commitment to your particular service, everyone involved will really begin to depend on you; and it will really develop you as a person."

If you have a service requirement at your school, look at it as a golden opportunity to help others and to gain skills that you can use in the future. Even students who initially dreaded their community service requirement have found volunteer work extremely rewarding. In fact, many of them continue to volunteer long after they've completed the hours necessary for graduation.

Ellie Grossman, a senior at The Brearley School in New York City, says, "Give a volunteer job several tries before you give up, because the first day can be difficult." Another New York City student, Charlie Bronstein, a junior at The Calhoun School, says, "Get involved with something you like, not just anything just to get it over with. And use your volunteering to get experience in a certain field."

I keep hearing that America is losing its competitive edge. Aren't there any American products that are still tops in the world?

Students who go abroad for the first time often are amazed to find that the products they take for granted at home are "hot commodities" in foreign lands. "Anything American, we like," said a Japanese foreign exchange student we met at New York University's student center. As a matter of fact, visitors to the United States are so enamored of American goods that a number of large department stores, as well as small, fashionable boutiques, have hired multilingual "personal shoppers" to assist foreigners in their money-spending endeavors. Tourists from abroad represent huge revenues in markets such as apparel and jewelry.

Even if you've never been out of the country, you're probably aware of American items that are all the rage overseas: Blue jeans, sneakers, cowboy boots, and college sweatshirts are just a few of the products foreign consumers can't get enough of. But in terms of U.S. exports, these products are just the tip of the iceberg. American industry continues to supply the world with some big-ticket items, as well.

Which foreign languages will be the most useful to know in the coming years?

Every American would benefit from learning one or more of the following languages: Arabic, French, Japanese, German, Chinese, and Russian. While the languages of business seem to be English, French, German, and Japanese, Arabic and Russian are fast becoming the common languages of diplomacy.

And those of you who know one of the major Chinese dialects will be in a good position when that sleeping giant wakens and flexes its muscles with the rest of the world.

As the world becomes a global marketplace, the American neglect of foreign languages is becoming more and more of a disadvantage. It's unlikely that English will be surpassed as the business and diplomatic communities' dominant language any time soon, but the quality of our interaction with our competitors and our partners will be vastly improved by a mutual understanding of one another's native tongues. If you want to be on the fast track in terms of career, learning a second or third language is one of the smartest moves you could make. And it surely would make traveling a lot more fun.

What do foreigners think of Americans and America?

Our friend George Gurley, a student at The University of Kansas, went on a mission on our behalf to answer this question. It was simple — he combed tourist traps in the Big Apple. He approached foreign students to find out what they think about real live Americans, the folks who swear by Mom, apple pie, and, yes, Chevrolets! Here's what they said:

•"Lots of conflicting ways of life, lots of contradictions between the people. Great split between rich and poor. Big differences between the cities. I've gone from San Diego to San Francisco and it was completely different, but everyone was nice. Here in New York, people don't talk. It's just work, work, work; time is money."

•"Americans. Hmmm . . . Lovable girls in California, not nice in New York. Lots of opportunities in the States it seems, but Italy's the fifth biggest economic power in the world. The U.S. has greater services like hospitals and transportation, and I think that this government is more concerned with its citizens, although I've seen a lot of homeless people today. There do seem to be a lot of work possibilities here for people who have not had very much education. In Italy one must be very educated to find meaningful work."

•"One thing I've noticed is that it's getting worse for lower-class people. That's very unfortunate. Now America is for older people and for higher-class people. It's becoming like Europe. In Japan there is more of a sense of community. There are also more necessities provided for the less fortunate."

•"I think American students are a lot freer to choose what they want to study."

What are the pros and cons of spending a year of high school abroad?

The prime advantage of living abroad during high school is that it offers you a unique opportunity to get to know what life is like in a foreign country. Victoria DeFrance, a junior at Harpeth Hall School in Nashville, Tennessee, has spent several summers in Australia, since her mother is a native of that country. Victoria says, "American teens and Australian teens get along very well because in lots of ways we're the same. Their schools are stricter, and kids wear uniforms, but when it comes to what's on their minds, we're thinking the same things." But even in countries that have cultures similar to our own, you'll find that the teenagers can be quite different from you and your friends at home. For example, in the United Kingdom it is unusual for a teenager to own a car. And it is much more common for teens to spend countless hours at the pub "at the end of the road" because the drinking age in England is fourteen and pubs are meeting places for people of all ages, especially outside of the big cities.

School life in foreign countries is different, too. While American high schools are almost like youth centers — places in which academics, social activities, sports, and volunteer work all merge — state schools in foreign countries tend to concentrate almost entirely on academics. And boarding schools throughout Europe tend to be more austere and traditional than their American counterparts.

N E W S F L A S H

Study-abroad locations that are currently the most expensive are England, France, Germany, and Japan. Least expensive: South America, Spain, Portugal, and most countries in Africa.

When we asked American exchange students what they liked least about studying abroad, we heard the same answer again and again.

Homesickness? Anti-American attitudes? A sense of alienation? Nope. Personal hygiene. That's right, it seems that America is home of the free and frequently bathed. Our standards of cleanliness are considered excessive in many parts of the world. A student we know who lived with a family in Stuttgart, Germany, complains that her hosts were nasty whenever she wanted to bathe or shower — apparently, electricity and hot water were resources the family wanted to ration. A young American who lived with a family in central Wales had a similar experience: "The only thing more controversial than my calling my family in Michigan, collect, was those weeks when I wanted to wash my hair more than just on Wednesday and Saturday."

Are there different types of study-abroad programs, or are they all similar?

Study-abroad programs fall into three main categories. There are those at foreign institutions in which English-speaking instructors teach classes according to the American system. There are those in which Americans attend foreign schools as regular students. And there are those in which special courses for American students are taught by native professors in the language of the country in which the program is located.

The type of program that would work best for you depends on how integrated you wish to feel in the foreign school. Some students feel left out of the "real" high school or university scene when they're in a program designed specifically for foreigners. But others feel uncomfortable being thrust into an entirely foreign academic setting — particularly when they're not fluent in the language. Your best bet will depend on the level of your fluency in the native tongue, the length of your stay, and the degree to which these academic credits are important to your record.

For more information about study-abroad programs, refer to *The Insider's Guide to Foreign Study: Everything You Need to Know About More Than 400 Academic Adventures Abroad*, by Benedict A. Leerburger (Addison-Wesley Publishing Company, Inc., 1987) and *Vacation Study Abroad*, edited by E. Marguerite Howard (Institute of International Education, 1989).

How will my education be affected if my family is transferred abroad?

Thousands of American teenagers and their families are living abroad. One of our co-authors, Alexandra Meckel, a freshman at The Spence

School in New York City, recently interviewed her childhood friend Jefferson Wilson, seventeen, who is in his final year at Bradford College, a boarding school in England. Jefferson attended Packer Collegiate Institute in Brooklyn Heights, New York, until the fifth grade; when his father accepted an overseas assignment, the family moved to London, England.

When Alexandra asked Jefferson about being an American at a boarding school that is almost exclusively English, he told her, "I always take the side of the country that I'm not then in. When I'm in England, I defend the United States." He does envision himself living in America when he's older and says that by the time he's in his thirties, he expects to be a lawyer and married with children. (Jefferson also said that his favorite pieces of Americana are *Catcher in the Rye*, "thirtysomething," *Dead Poets Society*, and the Grateful Dead.)

Here's Jefferson Wilson — in his own words — explaining the differences between English and American teens:

"English teenagers are far more concerned with fashion than are American teenagers. There is much more effort to be 'trendy' over here.

"The schools are far less liberal, although I'm mainly referring to the private schools (which, confusingly enough, are called 'public schools'). 'Masters' are what we call teachers, and they're usually addressed as 'Sir.' I wear a gown, similar to ones worn at American graduation ceremonies, to all morning classes and to Sunday chapel.

"There is also much more interest in current events and the government here — which America definitely could do with. Whereas Americans are concerned with themselves, English teenagers keep up with world events.

"At my school there is more drinking than at my American friends' schools — and probably more smoking. However, smoking is not allowed . . . and less drugs are present than at American boarding schools. I was amazed and shocked to learn that at a close friend's New England public high school, crack is regularly dealt out, although she is never involved and lots of other students aren't either.

"English teenagers are far more levelheaded and down-to-earth than their equivalent American dreamers. This comes from years of silenced jokes and childhood antics that are encouraged in America.

"But, behind these extremes of outgoing Americans and inward Englishmen and -women lies a hidden truth that only someone in my position can know for sure: Teenagers are teenagers."

(Postscript: Jefferson Wilson will be a member of the Class of 1995 at Bates College in Maine.)

hs adviser

On-Site Learning

A talk with Elaine Grossman, who spent one term of her junior year at Walt Whitman High School in Bethesda, Maryland, attending school in Israel:

How did you become involved with your program? What did the program entail?
I heard about the Alexander Mass High School in Israel through a friend of mine who had done the program and had told me how rewarding it was. I thought it would be a really good experience, which it turned out to be. It was eight weeks of living in Israel and taking two classes: History of World Civilization and International Relations. Two days a week were spent traveling to all of the historical sites and learning about history where it actually took place. The other days were spent in a normal classroom setting. There were about eighty Americans in my program, from all over the U.S. We lived in dorms at a school where there were also native Israeli students, as well as South Africans. If we wanted to stay with families, for weekends or whatever, there was a list made available to us of families who were willing to take us into their homes.

What did you like most about the program?
The best thing about the program was that I learned to like school. The teaching method was "classrooms without walls," and it really inspired me to want to learn. There were a lot of really great classroom debates and wonderful teachers. Also, I met so many interesting people. And I also really learned a lot about Judaism.

Go International at Home

So you want to host a foreign exchange student. Here are just a few of the organizations that have homestay programs that you and your family can become part of, usually at no cost except for room and board for your guest.

American Field Service (AFS)
1-800-237-4636
AFS is considered the Cadillac of the homestay programs — it is the oldest and among the most respected. Check to see whether your school already has a chapter, since many high schools do. AFS invites American families to host teachers as well as students.

The Experiment in International Living
(802) 257-7751
The Experiment has two homestay programs: Homestays in the U.S.A. and "Au Pair/Homestay U.S.A." The Experiment also offers some of the most innovative study-abroad programs for Americans, all of which include homestays.

Open Door Student Exchange
(516) 486-7330
Open Door offers programs involving students from the Americas, Europe, the Middle East, and Asia/Pacific and also has study-abroad programs for American students. The organization publishes a brochure for potential hosts. Call for your copy.

Youth for Understanding International Exchange
1-800-TEENAGE
YFU offers orientation programs and support from other host families, as well as publications designed specifically to help enrich participants' experiences. Each host family is assigned a YFU volunteer who's available to advise and help when necessary. P

College Talk

"It's such a relief to be accepted at my first-choice college, Bemidji State, in Bemidji, Minnesota. Now I know what I'll be doing next year — getting a good education, maybe in medical technology, having fun, and getting away from home."

Robin Reed, a twelfth grader at Washburn Senior
High School in Minneapolis, Minnesota

Q & A: CHOOSING THE SCHOOL THAT'S RIGHT FOR YOU

What role should my parents play in helping me select which colleges to apply to?

The only person who can pick the college that's right for you is you. Just because Dad and Mom rave about their days at the University of Texas doesn't mean you shouldn't consider other schools that might be more appropriate for someone of your abilities, aptitudes, and interests. After all, there are more than 3,000 colleges from which to choose, and you have a responsibility to yourself to make an informed decision.

That said, it's important to realize that the majority of parents don't insist on their kids' attending a particular school. But many of you will find that your parents do try to put limitations on the type of schools to which you may apply. The restrictions may be a result of financial constraints, distance from home, undesirable location (inner city, boondocks) unimpressive reputation, and so on. And sometimes your parents may oppose an entire category of schools. It can be a real problem if you're hoarding catalogs from Vassar, Oberlin, and Carleton, and your parents are singing the praises of Michigan, the University of Virginia, and the University of Indiana.

If you find that you and your parents are on entirely different wavelengths about schools, sit down and talk to them about it. Ask them what they think is so great about the schools they like. And listen to them. You may find they make a lot of sense. Then tell them what it is that excites you about the colleges on your "A list" — and be prepared to answer their objections. If it's a question of affordability, look into whether you'd qualify for financial aid and let them know you don't expect more from them than they are able to give. No matter what their reservations, your parents will be much more likely to accept your decisions if you can show that you've given the subject sufficient thought.

Colgate freshman David Portny saw firsthand just how important it is to insist on the right to make your own decisions concerning college. "I have one friend who allowed his parents to dictate the colleges to which he applied. What a fiasco senior year was for him — and now he's one of the few unhappy freshmen I know. You've got to be your own person, even if that means having difficult conversations with your parents about what it will take for you to be happy and successful. While you don't want to disappoint your family, it's important that you choose schools that are right for you."

What can I expect from a residential college? From a commuter school? What are their respective advantages?

A residential college provides an intense experience, and many people consider it the quintessential collegiate lifestyle. Because at a residential college you'd be responsible for every aspect of your well-being — from finding breakfast to acing your classes to making sure your clothes are clean — you're bound to do lots of learning just by living. If you have a choice of boarding at school or living at home, ask yourself the following questions: Do I wish that I were more independent? Do I wish that Mom and Dad took me more seriously and considered me an adult? Would I participate in extra classes, athletics, and/or extracurricular activities if I were able to? Are new friendships an important dimension of what I'm looking for in a college education? If your answer to most of these questions is yes, seriously consider spending at least your freshman and sophomore years in a dorm.

If money is an overriding factor, consider commuting. But be sure that your parents recognize that you're about to become a college student and that with the new responsibilities you'll be assuming, you deserve additional freedoms. Nevertheless, bear in mind that the age-old parental rule about following their rules when you live under their roof probably will still apply.

A student we met recently, at Morehouse College in Atlanta, Georgia, told us that he prefers to commute to school because at home he has the emotional support of his loving family — support that makes a big difference as he faces the heavy-duty pressure of premed studies. Another student we spoke to, at Bergen Community College in Paramus, New Jersey, says that her decision to commute was based entirely on financial considerations. "Before I decided to go to the community college," she says, "I thought about going away to school. Finances made that pretty much impossible, so I decided to make the best of a bad situation. I go to school every morning at 9:00 A.M. and stay until 4:00 P.M. I spend time in the library and at the gym and eat lunch in the student union frequently."

The student from Morehouse advises commuters-to-be to "make friends at school even if you spend most evenings socializing with old friends from high school. College is about meeting new people and trying out new ideas. If you don't meet lots of different kinds of people, how can you possibly try out different ways of thinking?"

I'm thinking about applying to a couple of women's colleges. What are the advantages and disadvantages of this type of school?

One of the main advantages of applying to a single-sex school in the 1990s is that you have a better chance of being accepted. Even the top women's colleges face competition for applicants from coed schools. This doesn't mean, however, that the education you'll receive won't be as good as, or in some cases even better than, what you would find at a comparable coed school. It does mean that you may have some advantage getting in. Rumor has it that if you think you are qualified for a good education but are not sure that your grades will get you into an Ivy League–level school, a top single-sex college may be your best bet.

Women's schools also continue to attract applicants who would have their pick of top-rated coed schools but prefer the advantages of a single-sex setting. Many students at women's colleges find that they are better able to express their individuality — both in and out of the classroom — in an all-women setting. They point out that they are much less likely to have to deal with sexual discrimination in the classroom and that they are never relegated to secondary status in math and the sciences or other traditionally male domains. And they find that the lack of male domination gives them the footing and confidence they need to assert themselves in the post-college world.

On the other hand, a single-sex setting isn't reality, and some students feel that it's too sheltered and gives insufficient preparation for the "real world." One student who transferred to a coed school after a year at a women's college says, "My fellow students were women who went to a single-sex college because they couldn't deal with men. Don't ask me what they're going to do when they get out into the working world and have to deal with men on a daily basis. Also, the social life stinks, no matter how much you road-trip to other schools. People think road-trippers from women's colleges are losers — out on the hunt for men." Another student from the same college raves about life there. "We have the best of both worlds: great teaching, a supportive environment, and there are always guys on campus. Within ten miles of this school, there are three large coed schools, so few people can't find male companionship."

Marcie Schorr Hirsch, director of career services at Wellesley College, agrees that a women's college is not for everyone. "But it is appropriate for a particular woman," she says, "especially one who has never been in an all-female setting for an extended period of time. The environment in a women's college is nurturing, one that helps students get their feet on the ground at a vulnerable time in their lives."

Admit One

Interview with Barbara-Jan Wilson, dean of admissions, Wesleyan University:

How should I go about choosing the school that's right for me?
The most effective approach is three-pronged. Start off by talking to people you know and gathering firsthand information on various schools. This is an excellent way to learn about what's out there. Once you decide which schools are of interest to you, send away for all published information about the schools and study it thoroughly. The third and most important step is the campus visit, during which you should begin to develop a "gut" feeling about whether or not the school is right for you. I strongly advise an overnight stay and a meeting with an admissions counselor in order to gain a broad perspective on the school and its atmosphere.

How can I "sell myself" to the school?
First of all, admissions officers are opposed to the belief that you must sell, or package, yourself in order to gain admission. This type of approach simply results in your looking superficial and very much like other applicants. Try to avoid this. You're better off pinpointing one thing that the admissions counselor should know about you and stressing that interest or accomplishment by supplementing it with related outside activities on your record.

Picking Winners

☆ It's never too soon to start thinking about college (unless, of course, you've started obsessing on a single institution by the first week of ninth grade). By junior year, when application deadlines are only months away, you should be able to narrow your selections to a dozen or so genuine possibilities.

☆ Okay, so you want to pick a winner — don't we all? One way to discover which schools are tailor-made for you is to conduct an interview — with yourself. Find out: What are your goals (both academic and career)? What sorts of programs will help you to realize those goals? Which schools have the courses, and the resources, you'll require? Continue the line of questioning: What will you major in? Does this major coincide with your career goals, or are you willing to put off career development until after college? How important is it to you that you have a "good name" on your diploma?

☆ Consider what kind of college environment you are looking for: small and intimate? midsize and manageable? large and sprawling? rural? suburban? urban? Would you prefer a less-intense environment in which cutthroat friends and neighbors aren't the norm? Could you be happy in a single-sex school? Would you be more comfortable at a school that has the same religious orientation as your own? Once you answer these questions, you'll be able to make a much more focused choice of schools to which to apply. (Hint: If a college has a promotion-al video, watch it carefully, as many of these questions will be answered over the course of its ten- to fifteen-minute duration.)

GETTING-IN TIP: "College fairs" and "college nights" can be helpful, but be aware that college representatives are there not only to distribute information but also to seek recruits. Don't expect a rep from college A to give you the real scoop on college B. And understand that the reps who visit may or may not have clout with the schools they represent. Sometimes alumni are asked to staff a booth at a college fair simply because they happen to live in the area. They don't necessarily have a lot of "pull" when it comes to recommending a candidate for admission. P

21

Getting into College

"When I think of college applications, I just want to fill them out as quickly as possible!"

Eddie Koterba, a senior at Omaha South
High School in Omaha, Nebraska

Q & A: THE INS AND OUTS OF THE APPLICATION PROCESS

I have my heart set on a certain college. How can I improve my chances of being admitted?

Don't succumb to admissions gimmicks. If you want to improve your chances once the application has been mailed, do the following: Improve your academic record, achieve in a major extracurricular activity, and stay in regular touch (but no more than once a month) with the admissions committee to let them know the seriousness of your interest. Don't send letters that say "Accept me." Instead, send a periodic update about your progress in school and about what's happening in your life.

Emphasize how you've taken charge of your life, the seriousness with which you're approaching life's latest challenges, and how well this philosophy will serve you when you arrive at That's the U for Me.

N E W S F L A S H

For information or a registration book for SATs or ACTs, write to the organizations directly: For SATs, write College Board Admission Testing Program, Box 592, Princeton, NJ 08541; for ACTs, write American College Testing Program, 2201 North Dodge Street, P.O. Box 168, Iowa City, IA 52243.

How involved should I let my parents be in preparing my college applications?

When your mother tells a neighbor, "We're applying to six schools," you know it's time to sit her down for a heart-to-heart chat. Let her know that, while you appreciate her concern and her input, applying to college is something you need to do on your own. Consult with your family and teachers about the application process. Bounce essay ideas off of them and let them evaluate your first draft. Practice mock interviews with them. But don't let them take over the entire process. Admissions officers have a keen eye for parental fingerprints. You're best off looking to your parents for good, sound advice. Nothing more, nothing less.

It's not always easy to convince your parents that you can handle something as important as applying to college. So show them from the start just how capable you are. A good place to start is the college tour. Even if your parents are paying for the trip and driving you from campus to campus, take charge. Make your own interview appointments. Select an appropriate outfit. Compile the data you'll need in order to fill out the forms you'll be handed when you arrive in an admissions office. It's as important that you show your parents you're mature as it is that you steer the course of your application process. This is an all-important time to establish yourself in your parents' eyes as a competent, thinking adult.

I've heard it's sometimes easier to get into college early decision. Is there any way colleges will find out if I apply early decision to more than one place?

Don't even think about it. Students who apply early decision to more than one school run the risk of destroying not only their chances of admittance but also their high school's reputation. Some colleges have been known to "punish" high schools whose students have reneged on an early-decision commitment.

Is it worth applying to a particular college if the top kids in my class are applying there as well? Would I be competing directly against them?

Sometimes there is no particular rhyme or reason as to who gets accepted where. Just because the other students have better grades than you doesn't mean they will definitely be chosen over you. Colleges look at a number of factors during the admissions process — grades are just one of them. When you know that the competition from your school is stiff, build a case for why you should be admitted without even acknowledging that you have competition on the home(room) front. An alumni interviewer for Cornell University says, "Please don't tell me about the other candidates' strengths and weaknesses, even if I slip and mention them by name. Be careful if you talk about students I may have interviewed in previous years, since I'm very sensitive about kids who put down others to make themselves look better."

There's no denying that most admissions committees compare you closely with others in the applicant pool who have backgrounds similar to your own. The best thing you can do in such an instance is to determine what makes you different. Then figure out how best to convey your special experiences, interests, and talents to a committee that is suffering from a heavy reading load and hundreds of applicants who sound very much the same.

A lot of colleges say I can write about anything I want in the personal essay. Any suggestions?

Write about something that moved you. The personal essay is no time to be blasé. Admit that you felt something and be descriptive enough so your readers will know what it was that affected you and what you gained from the experience. If you've had a rough childhood, tell them about it. Don't moan about the injustice of it all; describe, instead, what motivated you to keep thinking about the future. What gave you hope? Whatever you do, don't make the essay a bid for sympathy. A sob story is not going to get you anywhere.

If you choose to write about a death in the family or your parents' divorce, proceed carefully. Admissions committees are inundated by essays on these subjects. Write about this sort of experience only if you can show how it affected you in a positive way. Is this a life experience that matured you? Has it forced you to take on responsibilities unusual for someone your age? If not, you're better off choosing another topic.

151

If you write about your spring break in Bermuda, or at Snowbird or Vail, the committee may assume this is little more than boastful prattle. Write only about travel experiences that have had a powerful impact on you. Did you witness the dismantling of the Berlin Wall? Were you a volunteer with Habitat for Humanity in rural Mississippi? How did the experience affect you? What did you learn? Try to be insightful and positive. Dwell on the negatives only if they have moved you to positive action. Write creatively and always know why you are sharing the details you've chosen to include.

Once you've completed your essay, show it to older friends, parents, and/or teachers. But don't allow them to rewrite it. Nothing plays worse than an essay that looks packaged. The essay is the place in which to make the real you jump off the page and exclaim, "Take me!" Make the most of the opportunity.

I'm applying to a couple of schools that have a reputation for being full of liberals. Should I keep the fact that I'm president of the local Young Americans for Freedom off my application?

It is silly to make yourself into something you're not simply to appease or impress an admissions committee. Regardless of whether they have a reputation for being liberal or conservative, schools seek diversity, including diversity of opinion. Leadership achievement, in any legally and morally acceptable organization, is something you should be proud of. And it's certainly something that colleges look for in an applicant.

At the same time, it's not going to help your case if you approach the application process with an attitude of intolerance. Using the personal essay or interview as a platform from which to lambaste the school will win you few supporters. No matter how well thought out your arguments, the admissions officers are likely to remember your arrogance, not your critical thinking.

Show the colleges to which you're applying that you're a thinking, involved person. They'll respect that no matter which side of the issues you fall on.

Compiling the Perfect Record

Tips from Dorothy Swann, guidance counselor, Benjamin E. Mays High School, Atlanta, Georgia:

What advice do you give to students about compiling an impressive high school record?

I tell my students that the process of getting into college starts from Day One — the first day of high school. High school students have a "job," just like adults who go to work every day. If you do well at your "job," you will be accepted into a good college.

The first task for students at the start of each marking period should be to "plan" their report cards. On the first day of each class, the teacher distributes a syllabus outlining the content of that course. Based on that syllabus, the student should write down the grade that he or she plans to get in the class. This method has helped many of my students — once that goal is written down on paper, the students strive for it throughout the entire semester.

Another part of the students' "job" is to look at their schoolbooks not just Monday through Thursday, but Friday, Saturday, and Sunday as well. This doesn't mean that their entire weekends have to be spent in front of the books; with a realistic work plan there is plenty of time to relax. But studying consistently allows the student to come in each day — including Monday — and ask a sensible question of the teacher, very important not only for the learning process but for the teacher-student relationship, as well.

Counting Down to College

Applying to college is more than just a matter of filling out a couple of forms during senior year. If it's done right, the application process begins when you choose courses in your freshman year. The following are a few of the fundamental steps all college-bound teens should take.

Sophomore fall: finalize courses; read college catalogs to find out requirements at the type of schools to which you'll probably apply; commit yourself to extracurricular activities.

☆ Some schools encourage their tenth graders to take the PSAT. Therefore, why not spend a couple of hours a week during the summer between ninth and tenth grades getting prepped for the test? That way, you'll have a head start on the PSAT and know whether you'll need special coaching on the SAT.

Sophomore winter: register for Achievement Tests in subjects you'll be taking this year only (e.g., chemistry); make summer plans; consider hosting a foreign exchange student for summer or junior year.

Sophomore spring: take Achievement Tests; visit your guidance counselor to find out more about college admissions; plan a tour of colleges with your parents as an extension of family summer vacation plans.

Junior fall: sign up for and take the PSAT; have a college admissions planning session with your parents and guidance counselor once you've received your PSAT scores; increase your extracurricular and/or work commitments; develop a preliminary college list. Plan campus visits and write or call for information.

☆ Most colleges and universities accept the ACT in addition to — or instead of — the SAT. If you have a bent for science and social studies, the ACT can give you a chance to shine. The four subject areas of the ACT tests are English, math, science, and social studies.

Junior winter: study for the SAT/ACT; register for the SAT/ACT and Achievement Tests; visit college campuses and stay overnight in dorms whenever possible; make summer plans.

Junior spring: take the SAT/ACT and Achievements; complete initial college visits; meet with your guidance counselor to firm up your college list; begin to formulate answers to sample essay questions; practice interviewing so that you know what to emphasize about your background and interests and how to present yourself in the best possible light; talk candidly with your parents about financial matters so that you understand fully your financial-aid needs; sign up for senior year AP courses; finalize *worthwhile* summer plans and have a rationale for those plans.

Senior fall: retake the SAT/ACT and Achievements if necessary; take your AP courses mighty seriously; send away for college applications no later than September; schedule on-campus interviews wherever possible, also no later than September; secure teacher recommendations, especially if you intend to apply early decision; arrange for a peer recommendation since more and more colleges require these; sit down with your parents and fill out each college's financial-aid forms; complete applications, including essays; send in early-decision applications by November; prepare for alumni interviews.

Senior winter: last chance to retake the SAT/ACT and Achievement Tests; meet regularly with your guidance counselor to be sure that you're proceeding on course; submit regular-decision applications; make summer plans.

Senior spring: no later than March, send colleges a written update and your mid-year grades to let them know that you're a serious candidate; wait for the all-important mail beginning in late March; prepare for AP exams; if you're vacillating between two colleges, visit them once again; figure out what you want in a college roommate, because that form will be coming shortly; get set to graduate.

VOILÀ! High school is over. Get psyched for the big "C." **P**

22

Thinking About Careers

"I envision myself being a police officer or a lawyer, being married and having a wonderful and loving family."

Kirk Douglas Jolma, a twelfth grader at Monroe
Catholic High School in Fairbanks, Alaska

Q & A: CAREER OPTIONS FOR THE NINETIES

What if I'm doing okay in high school but I'm not interested in going to college?

Many skilled office employees are high school graduates who never attended college. They work in such areas as payroll, bookkeeping, purchasing, reception, secretarial, billing, and filing. If you think you'd like a career in business, find out whether your high school offers classes in typing, accounting, or other areas that will make you more employable. And, by all means, look for part-time or summer jobs in business. This experience will give you an edge when it comes time to hit the job-hunt trail.

If you're interested in pursuing a trade, your best bet is to obtain an apprenticeship in the field you're planning to pursue. This is how many skilled tradespeople learn their trades. Be prepared to commit yourself to at least two to four years of apprenticeship. And, although most of your training will be on the job, realize that you may be required to enroll in some formal classroom training — at a local school or community college. By the time the term of your apprenticeship has been completed, you will be a highly skilled tradesperson.

To be eligible for an apprenticeship, you should have a high school diploma or have taken an equivalency exam. Prior coursework in a technical subject is often recommended but usually is not required. To find out whether apprenticeships exist in the field in which you're interested, call a local labor union or a state employment office. Then contact employers in that field directly.

The following table shows just a few of the fields in which apprenticeships are available:

Field	Length of Apprenticeship (in years)
Automobile Mechanic	4
Bricklayer	3
Compositor	4
Floor Layer	3
Jeweler	3
Meat Cutter	2
Operating Engineer	3
Photoengraver	4
Tune-up Mechanic	2

For more information on ways to acquire a career education, contact The Job Corps, U.S. Department of Labor, Washington, DC 20210 or The Job Training Partnership Act, at the same address.

How does the job market look for the next decade for those who don't have college degrees?

Some of the fastest-growing occupations in the country don't require a college degree. These include positions as secretaries, nurses' aides, orderlies, janitors, sales clerks, cashiers, truck drivers, fast-food workers, general office clerks, waiters and waitresses, kitchen helpers, bookkeepers, construction helpers, automotive mechanics, supervisors, typists, licensed practical nurses, and carpenters.

The five fastest-growing high-technology jobs involve working as data processing mechanics, computer operators, computer analysts, office machine servicers, and computer programmers.

Why are some careers considered more prestigious than others?

In the recent past, money jobs — jobs in banks and brokerage houses and leveraged-buyout firms — were among the most glamorous. This was the case for two reasons: First, these jobs paid very high salaries. Second, these jobs allowed even the most junior personnel to feel as though they were part of history in the making because the deals on which they worked, and the companies and governments they financed, routinely were featured on the pages of the *Wall Street Journal* and other major newspapers. But times have changed. In the current market, financial jobs are losing ground to other, more secure positions.

The professions — accounting, law, and medicine — have been historically prestigious, perhaps because they have such rigorous educational and licensing requirements. Today, there is a glut of lawyers, but law school continues to be an appealing postgraduate option, especially now that money jobs are so much more difficult to land.

And medicine continues to attract recruits, despite requiring a particularly lengthy term of study. Tony George, a senior at Paramus Catholic Boys High School in Paramus, New Jersey, is applying to an accelerated medical program because, he says, "I'm worried about the cost and about the number of years I'll spend in school and training even if I'm admitted to a seven-year program." His classmate Vinod Paul is also applying to an accelerated program, a five-and-a-half-year medical college in India. "My career plan is to go into medicine, probably pediatrics, and if I don't get into an Indian med school, I'll go to Rutgers."

The degree to which a profession is considered prestigious varies from era to era and from country to country. After decades of second-class status in the United States, teaching has taken on new significance as an appropriate way to launch one's career. Young people's newfound interest in social service no doubt contributes to the popularity of this career option: Teach for America, a service corps of young college graduates, is a popular new program that appeals to those who want to make a difference in the lives of young people across the country.

International careers also are highly coveted. If you think that you want to go international, concentrate not just on economics and international relations but also on foreign languages and the social sciences — the better you understand people and what makes them tick, the easier you'll have it when you're rotated to Hamburg, Helsinki, or Hong Kong.

Are there such things as big-city careers, suburban careers, and careers for people who want to live in the country?

Many career counselors have begun to advise students to think about their career plans in the context of their life/work goals. Think about how and where you would be happiest living and what kinds of careers would enable you to realize your chosen lifestyle. Consider what sort of climate you prefer. Do you find the cold invigorating or paralyzing, or does it not seem to matter? How important are cultural activities to you? Would you feel cut off from society if you lived more than fifty miles from a ballet company or symphony orchestra? And also decide what sorts of people you most enjoy. Once you have an idea of the lifestyle you consider ideal, you'll be in a better position to choose a career that's compatible with those goals.

For example, if you love to ski and enjoy the brisk, outdoorsy life of the Mountain States or New England, you can still study law and join or start a practice in such places as Boise, Idaho; Missoula, Montana; or Concord, New Hampshire. But you might have to think twice about a career in advertising if those are the towns of your dreams.

If you're a natural entrepreneur, the exurbs, especially college towns, often are wonderful places in which to start small businesses, including retail establishments. If you love gourmet foods and you want to live a quiet life, why not consider opening a small shop in Columbia, South Carolina, or Athens, Georgia? You may not be able to meet your career goals right away, but you could begin learning the business by working in a store or as a caterer's assistant.

And there certainly are careers that pretty much require that you live, or at least work, in a big city. For example, if you're hoping to break into movie acting or international banking, you'll most likely find the greatest opportunities are in New York, Los Angeles, or some other large city. This doesn't mean you're stuck there for life, but it's probably a necessary step until you're established. If you're not sure about your career goals, but you know you want to live in the big city, your career planning certainly should include a serious look at finances. Life in urban America may be glamorous, but it isn't cheap. Don't plan to live the good life on an assistant editor's salary.

Wouldn't people be better off deciding how they'd like to live and then finding jobs that enable them to do just that?

We know a recent graduate of Bowdoin College who commutes to New

York City each morning from rural Washington state — by fax. While Ann's experience may be unique, there is a real lesson to be learned from how she has managed to work to live. Early on, you need to determine your life/work philosophy: Are you planning to work to live, or is your work going to be your life? Whatever your answer, focus on how you can maximize your chances of finding satisfaction by getting in touch with what you want from your career. Perhaps you don't even want a career; maybe you just want a job.

What are some career tips for the next decade?

•If you're bright and verbal and people-oriented, you may want to make a difference by making your career in the social services or teaching.

•If you care about the planet Earth and you're technically oriented, consider a career in environmental science or waste management.

•This is the decade in which to make your way as an entrepreneur. Careers for the millennium may well be service careers you conceive, initiate, manage . . . and make the most of.

•Assume that you must be computer literate regardless of where you want to work. Familiarize yourself with word processing and accounting software.

•Don't be unduly influenced by labor trends. By the time trends filter down to the average job hunter, those shortages featured in last month's news may well have been filled.

•Be prepared to work for foreign bosses. Consider learning Japanese, French, or German.

•Glamour jobs may offer sizzle, but have you ever tried to pay the rent with sizzle? Advertising agencies, the music industry, public relations firms, publishing houses, the television industry, and so on typically expect you to survive on the perks, rather than on the paychecks.

•The next twenty or so years are going to be the decades of the trades, of skilled craftspeople. Think long and hard about becoming a contractor, an electrician, a mechanic, or a plumber. These will be upper-middle-class jobs for the nineties and the early part of the twenty-first century.

hs adviser

An Alternative Route

Rachel Ribbeck, a member of the Class of 1988 at Lamar High School in Houston, Texas, who chose not to go directly to college, talks about her experiences:

I'm working as an aerobics instructor at the leading fitness studio in Texas, and I absolutely love it. I was active in aerobics all through high school, and I sort of knew all along that fitness was my forte. School was always hard for me, and I didn't enjoy it all that much. I didn't want to go to college, because I knew that I wouldn't apply myself. A few of my friends went to college right off the bat and ended up failing out and coming home to work. I think I kind of saved myself that wasted time.

It's been a good experience for me to be out in the working world. I think I've grown up a lot faster than some of my friends who are still in college. It bummed me out a little bit when they first were leaving for their freshman years, but, overall, I've been really glad about the decision I've made. I do think education is very important, and it's possible I'll go back to school to study physical therapy. But if I do make that decision sometime down the road, at least I'll know that it was well thought out and made from a more mature point of view than it would have been when I was eighteen.

Making the Right Moves

Career tips from Larry Simpson, director of career counseling, University of Virginia:

Lucrative jobs available to college grads in the nineties:

•Computer-related jobs

•Engineering positions

•Legal assistantships

•Sales and marketing positions

Steps to take in starting a career:

•Get experience — through internships or volunteering.

•Get to know people in your desired field. Talk to them about what they do. Network until you drop.

•Know yourself from an internal perspective. Self-awareness is very important in interviews.

•Send out resumés and cover letters — lots of them. P

Epilogue to High School

by Marian Salzman

A lot of you have asked me how my ten-year reunion was. Well, I have to admit, I didn't quite get there. I mean, I was well intentioned. I thought I'd go. But when many of my closest friends declined because they were living far, far away, it started to seem less important. It wasn't that I didn't want to see people, it was just that something about paying a hundred dollars a couple to eat Swedish meatballs and dance to your basic prom band didn't do anything for me at the time. Since then, I have regretted missing the party. (I did spend that night sitting in my apartment, listening to a tape of the "Best of the Seventies" music and rereading my yearbook, especially the messages my friends had penned to me so many years before.)

It's just that I didn't know what I'd say to people; I was sort of fearful that I'd go back and hate everyone or go back and love everyone or, most of all, that I'd go back and see high school for what it wasn't rather than for what it was. I worried that it just wouldn't be the same and that my pleasant memories might get recast.

My memories of River Dell Regional Senior High School are tied up in smells — mystery meat with gravy and mashed potatoes, Burger King Whopper Juniors, and Jontue perfume — and songs — Rod Stewart's "Maggie May," Al Stewart's "Year of the Cat," and just about everything by The Boss, Bruce Springsteen. I remember the Pine-Sol smell of the hallways and the grainy feel of the senior bench, where we sat after school, flirting, giggling, gossiping, and, every now and then, swapping class notes. I remember hanging out on the field behind the school. And I remember the way it smelled at high school football games when fall mingled in the air with Gulden's mustard and spicy hot dogs.

Afterword: What's Next?

Before you leave high school, take a good look around.

In ten years that total mouse in your English class may be the hottest-looking woman at your reunion. Okay, so right now it seems far-fetched, but a ten-year reunion is, well, years away.

And what's the only direct link you'll have between now and then? Your yearbook. That's right, that hardbound memento of this place and time is going to be a very well-read guide as you go forward to college, to life, wherever. Nine and a half years after you toss your cap into the air and kiss high school goodbye, you'll head to the attic, or at least to the back of your bookshelf, in search of *the* book.

Your best friend from high school will call — perhaps to reintroduce herself — and your mind will start to wander back. You might be Married . . . with Children or desperately seeking a mate or engrossed in a challenging career. In any case, nine-plus years have passed, and crow's feet have landed around your eyes. Or your hairline is receding — rapidly. Your spouse might be looking his age. Or you're about to head out on your 499th blind date . . . this year.

What do you expect your life to be like in ten years? Who do you plan to be?

Thank goodness that ten years from now you'll have a copy of the book that documents your innocence and confidence — the book that shines with your faith in a promising future. You'll open the yearbook to your pics, maybe even to a whole page devoted to the person you were, and you'll leaf through the rest of the pages, checking out your friends, your enemies, even the people you never bothered to know.

Whatever happened to the girl with pigtails — the one whose page features her at her first slumber party and on the arm of her prom date? She still strikes you as mighty attractive. Her family moved to Chicago, and you haven't seen her since graduation. Today, she's an English teacher or a cardiologist or an airline pilot.

What's become of the guy who sat next to you in calculus, the one who was shy, but, according to your then best friend, just a little sexy. The hometown network tells you he's on the fast track, an engineer, a guy who solves waste-management problems for a consulting firm down south. Your mother mentioned that his mother told her he's married — "to a nice girl, an attorney" — and that they've bought a house in Charlotte, North Carolina.

And what about the star football player and his girlfriend? They didn't marry — each other, that is. She married an older banker and lives in New York City, where she's a part-time script reader for a Broadway producer, a full-time mom to one, and a part-time stepmom to three. And he teaches at a prep school in Minneapolis. He married a fellow Peace Corps volunteer, but now they're divorced. He's gotten very spiritual — long gone is the rowdy frat boy who took Ohio State by storm in '92. Your mother heard he's thinking of moving back east, that he's considering entering a seminary. (Your mom has turned out to be a veritable pipeline of information about your classmates. Her regular visits to the supermarket are all that keep you from total oblivion.)

High school seems so long ago. George Bush was president. Saddam Hussein was enemy numero uno. (So much for your short-lived plan to work on a kibbutz for a year after high school — Mom still had the veto back then.) The Russians became our best friends just as SAT scores came back. And environmental awareness became the name of the game. The family dog was just a puppy then; today, he's an old guy who doesn't do much except eat his low-cal dinner and snooze in the entryway.

All the memories of today are captured in the book. Treasure it. Guard it when you get to college and your hallmates want to check out your friends. Guard it even when it seems to become less important, as you form new bonds and replace your longing for high school with your longing for college or for your friends from your first job.

And about that reunion . . . well, there's still plenty of time to diet and pump iron and write your success story. You have at least ten full years to get ready and set before it's time to go.

High School Is a State of Mind

"One of the things that worries me about the real world is not being taken seriously by adults. I want to be recognized for my accomplishments as adults do themselves. I'm scared of being disappointed in myself. And if family pressures, divorces, deaths of good friends, self-identity crisis, problems with friends, popularity, outside qualities, keeping up grades, refraining from skipping, smoking, drinking, and doing drugs isn't the 'real' world, then I don't know what is. It seems adults are so preoccupied with the thought that children are merely irresponsible and carefree that they're the ones who don't know what the 'real' world is. They don't realize that teens experience the same damn problems, yet it's just in a different form. They should awaken to not only their own reality, but to the reality of what teenagers really experience and who the hell they really are." —Blakely Nicole Braniff, an eleventh grader at Lamar Senior High School in Houston, Texas

"I dream of a place where resources are applied more efficiently in order to destroy or at least lessen the effects of poverty. I feel that human greed and injustice often take advantage of less powerful people. Most people need to be watchdogged." —Brian Ullmann, a senior at Shawnee Mission East High School in Prairie Village, Kansas

"I have, up until now, lived a very sheltered life. My parents are protective, and my school, which is small (350 people), is always there to help me with whatever problem I may have. I am worried that when I leave home and am forced to live independently, I will not be prepared for life's difficulties. People say that one's high school years are the best, and it frightens me to think that the times ahead will not be as wonderful." —Jessica Berkeley, an eleventh grader at Crystal Springs Uplands School, Hillsborough, California

"After I finish college, I hope to become a high school history teacher so I can help mold the minds of a generation that will be forced to make

major changes in society. I fear at the rate the world is going with military buildup and our deteriorating environment, we are on a head-on collision course with self-destruction. That's why I feel that teenagers must act now so that we will have a future." —James D. Loffredo, a twelfth grader at Grosse Pointe South High School in Grosse Pointe Farms, Michigan

"I am in eighth grade, and a lot of my friends like to hang out with the older kids at the high school. There is a lot of peer pressure from high school kids to do drugs. It's really important to stand up for what you believe in, and to be able to say no. I am trying to keep my head above water. It's important for me to do well in school, to please my parents and myself." —Amanda Abraham, an eighth grader at Garden City Middle School in Garden City, New York

"I am concerned about my future. The kids I know who are older than me never worried about their grades in ninth grade. Now they look back on it and wish they had cared. Therefore, I want to start off on the right path for college and to do well from the beginning. I am on the golf and volley-ball teams, and I am involved with the ski club. It's hard being a freshman and playing sports. I really have to try harder than the older kids so I can prove myself. I think a lot of freshmen hesitate to play sports because they know they are competing with the older kids. As far as substance abuse goes, I'm not involved. My friends respect me for being able to say no. They don't even bother me because I made a point from the beginning that I don't drink. It's important to make the right image initially." —Morgan Snyder, a ninth grader at Fox Chapel Area High School in Pittsburgh, Pennsylvania

"I am concerned about doing well from the very beginning of high school. I started worrying about college in the ninth grade. I am involved with extracurricular activities — I'm on the hockey and track teams. I really enjoy sports, but I also want to be a well-rounded person. Before entering the high school, I heard horror stories about the older kids. . . . I really want to do well because I have a lot of expectations for myself, and my parents and teachers also expect a lot from me." —Brian Schneider, a ninth grader at Highland Park High School in Highland Park, Illinois

About the Authors

Marian Salzman is the author of six books, including *War and Peace in the Persian Gulf: What Teenagers Want to Know* and *150 Ways Teens Can Make a Difference,* both for Peterson's Guides, and *Wanted: Liberal Arts Graduates* (Doubleday, 1987). She is managing director of the editorial services/marketing communications firm The Bedford Kent Group, of New York City and London. Salzman is a graduate of Brown University, Class of 1981, and River Dell Regional High School in Oradell, New Jersey, and has been editor in chief of *CV: The College Magazine.* She has been editor of *Management Review* magazine, and her writing credits include *Forbes, Ms.,* and *Self.* She has been featured in dozens of newspapers and magazines including *Business Week, Glamour,* the *New York Times,* the *New York Daily News, Savvy,* and *Women's Wear Daily,* and she is a regular guest on radio and television.

Teresa Reisgies is assistant editor at The Bedford Kent Group and a graduate of Georgetown University, Class of 1989. She is also co-author of *150 Ways Teens Can Make a Difference.* Teresa grew up in Alpine, New Jersey, and is a graduate of Tenafly High School in Tenafly, New Jersey. She lives in New York City.

Ann O'Reilly is a freelance editor and writer based in Washington state. She is co-author of *War and Peace in the Persian Gulf: What Teenagers Want to Know* and has been senior editor and copy chief of *CV: The College Magazine.* Ann is a graduate of Bowdoin College, Class of 1984, and the University of Denver Publishing Institute, Class of 1986. She grew up in New York City and Pelham Manor, New York, and is a graduate of The Ethel Walker School in Simsbury, Connecticut.

Amanda Abraham attends Garden City Middle School in Garden City, New York.

Ashley Bryan attends Episcopal High School in Belaire, Texas.

Caroline Portny attends The Spence School in New York City.

Dale Allsopp attends The Calhoun School in New York City.

David Portny, a graduate of Trinity School in New York City, attends Colgate University.

Marian Salzman

Teresa Reisgies

Ann O'Reilly

Amanda Abraham

Ashley Bryan

David Portny

Caroline Portny

Dale Allsopp

169

The following teenagers also contributed to this book:

Matthew Abbitt, Sebastian Abbot, Sarah Abbott, Margie Abdelrazek, Andrea Adams, Deanna Adcock, Kerston Ahren, Mary Brooke Akers, Cristy Alberton, Laura Allen, Allison Altman, Sumanth Ambur, Krissie Ames, Elizabeth Amory, Hallie Anderson, Sheana Anderson, Sherrelyn Kay Anderson, Brian Thomas Archibald, Charley Arensberg, Levilain Arnaud, Kati Asbury, Michelle Ashmore, Coleman Aster, Beyhan Atasoy, Jenny August, Thomas Ausye, Shannon Bachuss, Rebecca Bagatelle, Jody Bainbridge, Jessiva Banov, Tamara Michelle Baptiste, William Keith Barnhill, Anne Bartholomew, Jodie Bass, Daryn Batts, Kate Bauer, Tom Bayliss, Carl Beale, Kelly Beard, Tiffany Beauchamp, Kristine Beauregard, Michael Beck, Andrea Bell, Cary Bement, Dave Berg, Jennifer Berkeley, Danielle Berkley, Melissa Bernstein, Daniella Beznicki, Neil Bhargava, Robin Biderman, Jeff Bieker, Scott Billinger, Kathryn Black, Jonathan Blackmon, Ian Blakely, Ross Blank, Stephanie Blaylock, Mara Bodis-Wollner, Travis Boeve, Nancy Bollinger, Susan Bollinger, Shane Lynn Boney, Jon Borin, Lisa Borvegna, Kelley Bourke, Pam Bowler, Chris Bowles, Kate Bradbury, Dean Bradley, Blakely Nicole Braniff, Kathleen Brill, Cortney Brisson, Sheryl Brodeur, Anna Ruth Brown, Brittainy Brown, Cindy Brown, Debbie Brown, Janet Brown, Jennifer Brown, Sara Brown, Tania Brown, Woody Brown, Peter Brull, Leah Brunk, Todd Budlog, Brittany Bullard, Kristan Burch, Carrie Burn, John Bushore, Mae Byrd, Paul Campbell, Theodora Campbell-Urde, Brian Carl, Brad Carpenter, Rachel Carr, Laura Castin, Sarah Cate, Christina Cerrone, Gina Cerrone, Josh Chance, Kalyani Chandra, Carrie Chase, Courtenay Chilton, Jessica Chilton, Jimmy Chou, Courtland Pamela Christie, Scott Chueh, Sarah Chutiangtong, Beverly Clark, Gretchen Clark, Stephanie Clark, Court Clayton, Michael Coakley, Todd Coates, Lee Cole, Vickie Lynn Colvin, Ashley Compise, Mary Conner, Joe Conroy, Lydia Cook, Meredith Cooley, Christina Cooper, Susan Corbett, Elisa Marie Coscia, Jennifer Cosgriff, Jennifer Cox, Brad Cragin, Kathryn Crawford, Chad Creamer, Frankie Creech, Gigi Creed, Penny Creed, Kim Croce, Jason Crump, John Cunningham, Page Curry, Julie Custalow, Lauren Cutler, Sean Dailey, Stacie Dandrea, Leigh Danforth, Jessica Daniels, Molly Davenport, Joseline Davila, Alyson Lea Davis, Richard Carmen Davis, Chris Debnom, Amy Decko, Rachel DeCosta, Tiffany DeFrance, Helen Deftwiller, Tulloss Delk, Chad Depperschmidt, Hank Derby, Carol Anne Desgrosseilliers, Marty Desutels, Dabney Deswell, Melissa Devack, Manuel Diaz-Infante, Allyson Dimin, Amy Dinkel, Alexis DiStefano, Leah Dittoe, Bryan Doerries, Jessica Dollard, Scott Dolllard, Amy Dreuzs, Donna Driver, Brooke McLean DuBose, Holden DuBose, Steven Duchin, Laurel Duncan, Jen Eddinger, Ezra Edelman, Stacey Ehrlich, Kristin Eifert, Patrick Elison, Andrew Elliott, Allison Engel, Sarah Eppihimer, Kevin Everett, Amy Fahrenkopf, Jennifer Falik, Alison Fallon, Amanda Claire Farlee, Elizabeth Feld, Danielle Feman, Charles Ferlauto, Adam Paul Field, Jen Finley, Kristina Fisher, Genevieve Fitzgerald, Nora Fitzgerald, Patricia Ann Flake, Daniel Folmar, Anthony Fordham, Dave Forman, Chris Foster, Abby Fox, Hilary Fox, Jason Flax, David Frayner, Angela Cheryl Frederick, Anna-Lisa Freedman, Aparna Frenchman, Mieka Freund, Jeffrey Freundlich, Elizabeth Frieze, Gabe Fritz, Eric Futch, Kimberly Elizabeth Futrell, Rosa Gabriele, Heather Gadon, Vanessa Gaither, Erin Galbally, Katie Galbraith, Christoff Gallo, Kirsten Gardner, Claire Garrison, Kristen Gelinas, Jennifer George, Joe Geraci, Nathaniel Gerhart, Diana Gettinger, Lauren Giglio, Seth Gilbert, David Gilbertson, Bunny Girdler, Anne Glasser, Shannon Gnad, Jeff Godby, Rebeca Goldner, Sharon Goldstein, Jessalyn Gooden, Felicia Gordon, Keith Gorman, Selene Gorman, Ellen Grant, Missy Graves, Jen Greany, Ashley Green, Danni Green, Nichole Green, Victoria Green, Mark Greenblatt, Timothy Greenwood, Kyle Gregory, Jessica Griffith, Rebecca Miles Groody, Sharon Faith Groom, Martin Grubmueller, Miguel Guadalupe, Wendy Guilbert, Jennifer Haas, Elizabeth Hagan, Carol Hairfield, Maura Hanenbaum, Kate Happer, Lucas Terrell Hardee, Chris Hardison, Sophia Hardy, Christine Hargrove, Nick Harkeem, Kelly Renee Harrell, Kassy Harris, Ross Harris, Mike Harrison, Chrissie Hart, Julie Harting, Jason Hartline, Jeff

Harvey, Emily Hatch, Amy Hauser, Emily Wendel Haynes, Mike Hebb, Donnie Hebert, Jon Hegarty, Rebecca Heller, Danielle Anitka Helm, Staci Hemstreet, Mina Henriksen, Robin Hensarling, Dan Herzig, Suzette Higgins, Susan Hittner, Diane Avery Hockstader, Heather Elaine Hodde, Stuart Hodgeman, Jonathan Hodgman, Kevin Holliday, Shelley Holman, Jason Holmes, David Holt, Nate Holtberg, Brandon Hornton, Bar Horowitz, Maia Horta, Adam Wayne Houston, Tommy Howard, Evan Howell, Judith Howell, Laurin Howell, Matthew James Hubbard, David Huber, Leslie Huddleston, Gerard Huot, Amy Mareen Hutchens, Andrew Immerman, Christina Isaly, Elena Jacobson, Mary Catherine James, David Jasper, Joy Jaworski, Marisa Jennings, Luke Johnson, Alecia Johnson, Heather Johnson, Kathy Jones, Tara Jones, Troy Byron Jones, Whitney Jones, Victoria Kahn, David Kang, Jeffrey Katz, Mandy Kellener, Andrew Keller, Sharon Kelley, Dwight Keysar, Braun Kiess, Jim Killam, Shilla Kim, Terry Kinderknecht, Heather King, Jessica King, Lauren Kim, Mary Pillow Kirk, Kris Kirkman, Frank Kisselt Jr., Melissa Kitley, Allison Kittredge, Crissa Klein, Carrie Kline, Tiffany Knight, Amy Knowles, Nora Kobos, Scott Kohl, Kelly Koltes, Helen Korcoulis, Jarrett Kovics, Robbie Kravitz, Sean Kreps, Isabel Kriegel, Jessica Kron, Karen Kuhn, Nick Kukulinski, Elizabeth Kyger, Merrill Lackey, Becky Lamb, Helena Lamb, Lisa Lancaster, Elena Laskin, Jeff Latchum, Christopher Lavallee, Alli Lavenstein, Charles Hammond Lawton, Stephanie Lazar, Chris Leadbetter, Brittani Lee, Todd Lefkowitz, Jason Legleiter, Sasha Lehman, Marc Leiker, Melissa Lerner, Patrick Lerner, Adina Lessen, Sandi Levin, Caren Levinson, Abraham Levitan, Jacqueline Lewis, Greg Licht, Jodi Liebman, Suzi Lipman, Aumomaleahh Livingstone, Fred Longwood, Diana Lorenz, Aimee Losey, Elexis Loubriel, Amy Lowen, Emily Loyd, Libba Loyd, Doug Lucas, Jennifer Luil, Amy Luysterborghs, Elizabeth Lynch, Tara Lynch, Christyna Macbeth, Sarah Catherine MacMahon, Jamie Macon, Paxton Madison, Marc Madonia, Melissa Maeurer, Camilla Elizabeth Mager, Jessica Malman, James Malone, Jose Miguel Mantilla, Elena Marcuss, Lauren Marler, Christopher Marlowe, Cynthia Ann Marlowe, Jessica Marrero, Courtney Marshall, John Marshall, Beth Martin, Jimmy Martin, John Ingle Martin, Chris Maser, Margot Matouk, Kate McCall, Sara McCall, Effie McCandless, Karen McCarthy, Shawn McCarthy, Monique McCloud, Monica McCollin, Julie McDonald, Julia McFerrin, Georgette McGill, Colin McGrath, Keisha McKenzie, Kristin McKinley, Madie McKnight, Becki McLamb, Deborah McNamara, Dean McNeely, Lindsey Mead, Sean Meehan, Robyn Metcalf, Steven Michaud, Eddie Miller, Shannon Miller, Stephanie Miller, Mollie Mills, Phillip Mills, Ashley Miner, Paul Miner, Amanda Minker, Jesse Mishler, Tom Mister, Laurie Moldawer, Vanessa Montgomery, Lauri Mary Lea Montoya, Cory Moore, Leslie Moore, Claudia Moran, Katie Moran, Lauri Anne Moreau, Dion Morning, Maria Morrissey, Nicole Mosca, Adam Mozo, Aaron Mulder, Shannon Mullen, Bobby Murphy, Marc Murphy, Meghan Murphy, Stratton Murphy, Donna Murray, J. Nan, Maya Narula, Richard Nash, Sarah Nash, Nancy Nava, Tony Neal, Andy Nelman, Dana Nerenberg, Jill Marie Neuburger, Tyler Newby, Michelle Newman, Bobbs Nishikawa, Caroline Nixon, Kelly Nordlinger, Eddie Norman, Nadjwa Effat Norton, Tahira Adar Norton, Christie Joy Nudelman, Tennille Neuharth, Monica O'Brien, Kristin O'Connell, Rachel Obenzinger, Julie Ober, Allison Stephanie Ohlgren, Jason Oliver, Christina Olsson, Lindsey Orcult, John Orders, Lisa Otsubo, Erika Angela Otue, Sean Graham Outlaw, Kazuyoshi Ozawa, Kathryn Ozier, Abby Parker, Sarah Parker, Allison Parks, Meredith Parks, Emily Kern Pasler, Blake Patterson, Pamela Ann Petras, Sarah Petrell, Lainie Petrie, Tara Pfannenstiel, Tim Pfannenstiel, Chad Phelps, Tracy Phifer, Jason Phillips, Sarah Phillips, Mary Alice Pickert, Elizabeth Piggott, Emily Pollock, Natalia Porcelli, Martin Pozanski, Christi Pratt, Tom Presciotta, Cynthia Price, Reid Prichett, Josephine Proctor, David Provencher, Tracy Pruzan, Sammy Putnam, Jennifer Quackenbush, Stephanie Rafael, Katherine Rapaczynski, Michele Rattien, Joe Raymond, Alex Raziz, Marnie Reasor, Dhruva Reddy, Jami Reever, Rachel Reeves, Kelly Regan, Andrew Reis, Amy Renner, Brandy Richards, Heather Richards, Jeff Richmeier, Lorraine Riddell, Louise Riddell, Lisa Riedel, Rachel Ritchie, Brad Rivenbark, Michael Robert, John

Michael Robertson, Jim Robinson, Lee Robinson, Melanie Robinson, Alexandra Roisen, Jeff Rome, Julianna Kate Rosenbluth, Win Rosenfeld, Abby Rosner, Amanda Lane Rouse, Richard Royal, Anderson Lee Royston, Emily Rubenstein, Heather Rucker, Karrie Ruda, Elizabeth Rumbold, Noah Russell, Rebecca Russell, Shawn Russell, Jake Ruttes, Andrew Sanford, Jason Sanborn, Douglas Saphies, Bryan Scott Sapp, Katie Scaglione, Kevin Scanlon, Sarah Scarborough, Tara Scarlett, Ellie Schilling, Jody Schmidt, Leslie Schmidt, Megan Schneebaum, Jonathan Schneidler, Jon Scholnick, Mike Schuler, Barry Schumacher, Meredith Scouille, Matt Seiff, Elisha Sessions, James Sewell, Adam Shapira, Ian Shapira, Mary Sharp, Alex Sherman, Kate Sherrard, Joshua Shimkin, Amy Siegel, Wendy Siemens, Mike Silberstein, Eric Sillman, Jim Simpson, Vicki Siokis, Sunitha Siva, April Slensky, Curtis Sloane, Amy Smallridge, Allison Smith, Dwight Stuart Smith, Katherine Smith, Cecil Smyth, Beth Snyder, Nicholas Snyder, Maisie Sokolove, Leah Spencer, Jennifer Spinella, Adrienne St. Onge, Ilisa Stalberg, Christy Stallings, Elizabeth Steffen, Amy Stein, Stuart Steinbock, Caroline Steinert, Somer Stephenson, Eric Stevens, Jennie Stevens, Tiffany Stevens, Jessi Stockdale, Miles Edwin Stocker, Phil Stockl, Melissa Stone, Blake Stone-Banks, Kathleen Stoney, Margaret Streicker, Stephen Strickland, Erin Sullivan, Garth Svenson, Laura Swain, Taylor Lauren Swanson, Collier Swecker, Brian Taylor, Donna Teachey, Amie Tessler, Von Tettleton, Laura Thomas, Joseph Thompson, Rena Thompson, Ian Thorson, Matt Tierney, Daniel Todd, Myka Todman, Jeff Tolbert, Lisa Tompkins, Lisa Torrisi, Jennifer Towbin, Matthew Tramp, Gene Treener, Jennifer Tripett, Kristin Triplett, Tom Tsai, Derek Turbide, James Tuschman, Maggie Uden, Shay Upadhyaya, Yarrow Upton, Jeff Vanderslice, Mary Vanie, Akin Vaughan, Matt Vaughan, Aaron Vigneault, Jodi VonLintel, Richey Wagner, Bill Waite, Allison Wales, Kathryn Walker, Tom Wallace, Courtney Walter, Sarah Walton, Allison Wanger, Tokesha Warner, Jordan Watson, Libby Weaver, Lisette Weaver, Ryan Weisiger, Linden Weisman, Andrew Weiss, Julie Weiss, Robinette Weiss, Keelyn Welch, Andy Wells, Dean Burke Wells, Shannon Wertin, Kara West, Sally Westlake, Anne Wheeler, Christine Whelan, Alex White, Stephen Whitehead, Miller Wild, Anna Williams, Hunter Williams, Jody Wilson, Kelly Wilson, Jodi Wilt, Synne Wing, Gillian Wollen, Kala Wright, Vanessa Wruble, Amy Yaeger, Ken Yamamoto, Grace Yang, Siti Yearwood, Bettina Yip, Holton Yost, Charles Young, Jessie ZeMars, Diana Zicklin, Jessica Zimmerman, Mary Zink, Mike Zucker, Joanna Zurada, and Bryant Zwart.

Index

MEET THE CO-AUTHORS (see back cover)

1. Alieda Hempstead, 2. Nancy Wong, 3. Zoe Schonfeld, 4. Dana Wolf, 5. Amanda Abraham, 6. Alexandra Marrufo, 7. Tara Bradley, 8. Adam Kanner, 9. Mindy Jones, 10. Alexandra Meckel, 11. Melissa Marshall, 12. Ashley Bryan, 13. Sarah Ribbeck, 14. Kathryn Alexander, 15. Victoria DeFrance, 16. Jamie Stover, 17. Alex Quintero, 18. Meredyth Cohn, 19. Tracy Weinberg, 20. Dale Allsopp, 21. David Portny, 22. Kyle Galloway, 23. Caroline Portny, 24. Joey Schmidt, 25. Adam Goodman, 26. Ryan Nelson, 27. Brian Klugman, 28. Rebecca Stevens, 29. Leo Shin, 30. Dan Diman, 31. Meraiah Foley, 32. Jamie Sattel, 33. Kirk Kenfield, 34. Jeff Toohig, 35. Matthew Thanner, 36. Maria Rosel, 37. Toi Jones, 38. Emily Miller, 39. Jessica Berkeley, 40. Andrew Hunter, 41. Tony George, 42. Lawrence Thaler, 43. Bryan Thanner, 44. Colin Robinson, 45. Vinod Paul, 46. Ron Palmon.

Alphabetical key:

If you would like to be considered for future National High School Reporter™ programs, write to:

Marian Salzman
The Bedford Kent Group
156 Fifth Avenue, 8th floor
New York, NY 10010

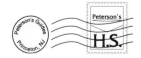